THE LYRIC AND DRAMATIC

Milton

THE LYRIC AND DRAMATIC

Milton

SELECTED PAPERS FROM THE
ENGLISH INSTITUTE

Edited with a Foreword by JOSEPH H. SUMMERS

COLUMBIA UNIVERSITY PRESS
New York and London   1965

Acknowledgment is made to The Macmillan Company, Macmillan & Co., Ltd., and Mrs. W. B. Yeats for permission to quote
three lines from "Crazy Jane Talks with the Bishop," by W. B.
Yeats. Copyright 1933 by The Macmillan Company; renewed
1961 by Bertha Georgie Yeats.

*The frontispiece and title page of the 1645 volume of Milton's
poems are reproduced through the courtesy of Yale University
Library.*

FOREWORD

Many readers of *Revaluations* in the 1930s may have felt that F. R. Leavis' judgment about Milton's reputation ("Milton's dislodgement . . . was effected with remarkably little fuss") was a bit premature—although, at the time when Leavis wrote, there was a good deal of evidence for his opinion. But surely few of those readers could have anticipated the present "Milton revival," when more essays and books are published each year on Milton than on any other figure in English or American literature except Shakespeare. Most of the current critical judgments of Milton's poetry seem to indicate that the "general critical climate" (if one can speak of such a vague abstraction) is as favorable to Milton today as it has ever been since the eighteenth century.

It is easy to overdramatize what has happened. Despite all the publicity, there was never, of course, a time when everyone disliked Milton. When the hostile judgments of Eliot and Leavis were most influential, many students of Charles Williams, C. S. Lewis, Douglas Bush, and others—in addition to unorganized readers, young and old—continued to find delight in reading

10671

Milton. (We may need to remind ourselves, too, that, despite the current "revival," there are still intelligent readers who, for one reason or another, cannot read Milton with pleasure.) Many students in the earlier period were more or less convinced by the popular theorists that, "for our time" at least, the "dramatic lyric" was the chief poetic form, that all poetic styles should aspire to the colloquial if not the angry or passionate, and that sensory and psychological "realism" was the chief value one could expect from literature. Still, a number of them discovered that their experiences in reading Milton were difficult to square with their theoretical allegiances. Perhaps what has happened is merely that the discovery of such a gap between experience and theories is now so general that many readers feel compelled to work out new theories—or to rediscover old ones.

Paradise Lost has been, naturally, the big "discovery," but it has been pointedly excluded from this volume. With so many studies published recently (and with other distinguished volumes to appear shortly), an additional group of disparate essays on that epic seemed hardly to the point at this time. Instead, the Supervising Committee of the English Institute planned two conferences on poems of Milton which have recently received less, if only slightly less, attention. The first three papers in this volume were delivered in 1964 as part of the conference on *Poems of Mr. John Milton* (1645) which Professor Louis Martz directed. In 1963 I directed the conference on *Samson Agonistes,* which consisted of the last three papers. The effect of the resulting volume is, at first and perhaps at second glance, odd: those first essays on Milton's first "Selected Poems" and the last three on the last published poem, with the large gap in the middle where the two epics should be. Of course the "lyric and dramatic Milton" is not the "whole" or even the most distinctive Milton. But aside from matters of timing and necessity (and it would take a volume much larger than this to represent significantly the current lively writing on *Paradise Lost* and *Paradise Regained*), the arrangement of the volume may point up a few things which today's readers of Milton sometimes forget. *Poems* (1645) did establish the fact, for any contemporaries who cared about such things, that Milton was the best English poet living at that date. *Samson Agonistes* is one of the very few dramatic poems in English which, without embarrassment, we can profitably compare with the Greek tragedies. If Milton had written only the poems discussed in this volume, he would still be recognized as one of the two or three supreme artists in English poetry. However inevitable it is for most of us to concentrate our attention on *Paradise Lost* and to note the early anticipations and the later echoes of that great poem, we can profit from the attempt to look at the other poems—in their own right—as directly and as carefully as we can.

In the first of the three essays on *Poems* (1645) (this volume was actually published in January of 1646 according to modern dating), Professor Martz provides a fresh look at the volume as a whole—its carefully presented promise and variety and achievement—and directs our attention particularly to the first major poem, *On the Morning of Christ's Nativity*. In his consideration of *Comus,* Professor Barber demonstrates that, instead of being an unsuccessful "drama," the poem is a successful masque, of which an alert and imaginative reading may discover the continuing delights. In the final essay of the group, Professor Mac-Caffrey has written what one might well have thought impossible at this date: an informed reading of *Lycidas* which, without eccentricity, communicates new insights in a moving fashion.

Although the last three essays are concerned with the same dramatic poem, they differ from each other more obviously in method and approach than do the essays of the first group. Professor Madsen shows the light which his long-range interest in Milton's use of Christian typology can cast on *Samson Agonistes*. In his careful consideration of the verse, both the problems of its origins and the problems of how we are to read it aloud, Professor Weismiller gives us an exciting anticipation of his full treatment of Milton's verse in the forthcoming Variorum Commentary. In my own essay I attempt to describe some of the movements which make the drama, and particularly the manner in which the Chorus directs our attention to those movements.

The six essays printed here represent no "school." They are not much concerned with establishing a new literary "orthodoxy," either in criticism or in scholarship. What they have in common, however, is important: they are written by six teachers who like to read Milton, who seem to find his poetry continually interesting, and who are still attempting to find out more about it—its language, its ideas, its sounds and rhythms, its conventions and innovations, its full literary and historical contexts—its "meanings" for a hypothetically intelligent and sensitive contemporary of Milton as well as for an intelligent and sensitive reader in our own time. All the authors of these essays are interested in the *experience* of reading Milton's poetry. I believe that most readers with a similar interest—or perhaps merely with curiosity about it—will find these essays useful.

It may be too much to expect, but one hopes that the "Milton revival" will continue along the rather loose, undogmatic lines suggested by this volume. Of course we need more accurate scholarship: there is no virtue in suspending judgment about determinable matters of fact, and no valuable "richness" results from the continuation of demonstrably false notions or interpretations. But no one who really admires Milton's poetry and who knows something of the way works of literature live can look forward to a uniformly "correct" evaluation of the poetry. Uniform judgments only occur about literary works which are near to or have arrived at the point of death. So long as informed and intelligent individuals continue to *read* Milton, they will not find themselves agreeing about all the "decorous" responses and evaluations. At the moment the poetry of England's most ambitious poet seems splendidly alive.

JOSEPH H. SUMMERS

Washington University
St. Louis, Missouri
January 27, 1965

CONTENTS

I

POEMS OF MR. JOHN MILTON (1645)

Louis L. Martz

THE RISING POET, 1645

. . . as true a Birth, as the Muses have brought forth since our
famous *Spencer* wrote; whose Poems in these English ones are
as rarely imitated, as sweetly excell'd.
     Humphrey Moseley, "The Stationer to the Reader"

It is hard to maintain a clear view of Milton's volume of 1645,
since the annotated editions that we are most likely to be using
have broken up Milton's generic groupings and have rearranged
these poems in chronological order, interspersed with other poems
that Milton did not choose to publish here. I do not mean to
quarrel with these rearrangements, which have the advantage of
allowing one to trace accurately the development of Milton's
early poetical career. And indeed Milton himself has taken the
lead in making such a view of his career possible, since his volume of 1645 takes care to date many of the poems and arranges
them in rough chronological order, within the various genres
represented. Yet Milton's attention to genre makes an immense

difference, for it asks us to view the poet's development according to the principles of poetry: it asks us to look upon the writer in a special aspect. Milton's original arrangement creates the growing awareness of a guiding, central purpose that in turn gives the volume an impressive and peculiar sense of wholeness. In order to regain the significant integrity of the volume one must, now and then, go back to the original.

Perhaps the best way into the volume is to follow Milton's own description of it, in the Latin ode that he sent in January, 1646–47, to John Rouse, Bodley's Librarian, with a copy of the book. This is a mock-heroic poem of remarkably high spirits, written in an unprecedented form that MacKellar calls a "metrical experiment or jest." [1] The manner is one of learned wit that makes translation almost impossible; I give here a composite version drawn from Hughes and McCrae,[2] with intermittent comments:

"Book in twin parts, rejoicing in a single cover, yet with a double leaf" [that is, as the general title page says, these are "Poems of Mr. John Milton, both English and Latin," with a separate title page for the Latin poems and separate pagination for the English and the Latin parts; the "double leaf," however, not only alludes to the two title pages, or the two parts, but at the same time suggests the double wreath of laurel that the poet has won for his performance in two languages], "and shining with unlabored elegance which a hand once young imparted—

[1] *The Latin Poems of John Milton,* ed. Walter MacKellar (New Haven, 1930), p. 358.
[2] *John Milton: Complete Poems and Major Prose,* ed. Merritt Y. Hughes (New York, 1957), p. 146. See the translations of the Latin poems by Nelson G. McCrea in *The Student's Milton,* ed. Frank Allen Patterson (New York, 1930), p. 109.

a careful hand, but hardly that of one who was too much a poet—" [that is, not yet a master-poet] "while he played, footloose" [*vagus,* "wandering"], "now in the forest-shades of Ausonia and now on the lawns of England" [*Ausonias umbras:* the phrase may be taken to include a reference to his own Italian journey, to the poems in the Italian language, to the Latin poems, and to the pervasive atmosphere of Greek and Roman pastoral that plays throughout the volume: Ausonia includes Magna Graecia], "aloof from the people, and forsaking the common paths, he indulged his native lute, and presently in like fashion with Daunian quill called forth for his neighbors a melody from far away, his foot scarcely touching the ground" [*pectine Daunio:* the song and instrument of ancient Italy].

Here is the picture of a youthful poet, free from adult cares, sometimes wandering alone, amusing himself, sometimes making music for his friends or acquaintances, sometimes writing in his native vein, sometimes evoking a strain from idealized antiquity —but with a light and dancing posture that we do not usually associate with John Milton: *et humum vix tetigit pede.* It is clear, from many indications, that Milton has designed his book with great care to create this impression.

The entire volume strives to create a tribute to a youthful era now past—not only the poet's own youth, but a state of mind, a point of view, ways of writing, ways of living, an old culture and outlook now shattered by the pressures of maturity and by the actions of political man. Even the frontispiece, by William Marshall, attempts to set this theme. The aim of the engraving is clearly to present the youthful poet surrounded by the Muses,

with a curtain in the background lifted to reveal a pastoral landscape of meadow and trees, where a shepherd is piping in the
shade, while a shepherd and a shepherdess are dancing on the
lawn. The legend around the portrait identifies it as a picture
of the poet in his twenty-first year—but in fact the portrait presents the harsh and crabbed image of a man who might be forty
or fifty! Marshall could do better than this, as his engraving of
the youthful Donne testifies; one almost suspects deliberate
sabotage here.[3] If so, Milton performed slyly an appropriate revenge. For under the portrait, neatly engraved in Greek—engraved no doubt by Marshall himself—we have the following
comment by Milton:

> That an unskilful hand had carved this print
> You'd say at once, seeing the living face;
> But, finding here no jot of me, my friends,
> Laugh at the botching artist's mis-attempt.

With this learned practical joke, the volume begins in high spirits;
how can we doubt, after this, that Milton had a considerable
sense of humor?

Meanwhile, the facing title page prepares us for a volume that
will contain songs of unlabored elegance, in the recent courtly
style: "The Songs were set in Musick by Mr. Henry Lawes
Gentleman of the Kings Chappel, and one of His Maiesties

---

[3] See the amusing account in David Masson's *Life of Milton* (7 vols., London,
1859–94), III, 456–59; Masson sees in a passage of *Tetrachordon* a pun on
Marshall's name. The translation of the Greek verses below is that of Masson,
III, 459.

Melpomene.   Erato.

Prin:

IOANNIS MILTONI

ANGLI EFFIGIES

ÆTATIS   vigesis

ANNO

Urania.   Clio.

Ἀμαθεῖ γεγράφθαι χειρὶ τήνδε μὲν εἰκόνα
Φαίης τάχ᾽ ἄν, πρὸς εἶδος αὐτοφυὲς βλέπων·
Τὸν δ᾽ ἐκτυπωτὸν οὐκ ἐπιγνόντες φίλοι
Γελᾶτε φαύλου δυσμίμημα ζωγράφου.

W·M· sculp:

POEMS

OF

Mr. John Milton,

BOTH

ENGLISH and LATIN,

Compos'd at several times.

Printed by his true Copies.

The S o n g s were set in Musick by
Mr. H e n r y   L a w e s Gentleman of
the K i n g s Chappel, and one
of His M a i e s t i e s
Private Musick.

——— Baccare frontem
Cingite, ne vati noceat mala lingua futuro,
Virgil, Eclog. 7.

Printed and publish'd according to
ORDER.

LONDON,
Printed by *Ruth Raworth* for *Humphrey Moseley*,
and are to be sold at the signe of the Princes
Arms in S. *Pauls* Church-yard. 1645.

Private Musick"—a notice quite in line with Moseley's preface, which associates Milton's volume with the poems of Waller that Moseley had published a year before. Waller, as everyone knew, had been exiled for his plot against the Parliament on the King's behalf; nevertheless Moseley insists on saying: "that incouragement I have already received from the most ingenious men in their clear and courteous entertainment of Mr. *Wallers* late choice Peeces, hath once more made me adventure into the World, presenting it with these ever-green, and not to be blasted Laurels." This bland ignoring, or bold confronting, of the political situation, with its emphasis upon the transcendent values of art, is maintained by reprinting here, from the 1637 edition, Henry Lawes's eloquent dedication of Milton's *Mask* to a young nobleman with strong Royalist associations; by the Latin poems in memory of the bishops of Winchester and Ely; by the complimentary writings prefixed to the Latin poems, showing the high regard that Milton had won in Catholic Italy; by Milton's admiration for Manso, the fine old Catholic patron of Tasso; and by other aspects of the volume, notably the sonnet beginning: "Captain or Colonel, or Knight in Arms,/ Whose chance on these defenceless dores may sease." This is not a poem of presumptuous naïveté but of mature awareness, in which the poet, as Brooks and Hardy say, with a "wry humor . . . contemplates, a little ruefully but still with a fine inner confidence, the place of the poet in a jostling world of men at arms." [4]

---

[4] *Poems of Mr. John Milton: The 1645 Edition with Essays in Analysis,* by Cleanth Brooks and John Edward Hardy (New York, 1951), p. 157. This valuable edition includes only the English poems, with a very helpful commentary on each poem.

Lift not thy spear against the Muses Bowre,
　The great *Emathian* Conqueror bid spare
　The house of *Pindarus*, when Temple and Towre
Went to the ground: And the repeated air
　Of sad *Electra's* Poet had the power
　To save th' *Athenian* Walls from ruine bare.

But will the King's Captain do the same for one who is not yet
"too much a poet"? There is room for doubt, and hence the plea;
but no doubt at all about the power of poetry and this poet's
hopes to achieve the immortality of Fame. He has told us this
through the motto on the title page, there identified as coming
from Vergil's seventh eclogue:

───Baccare frontem
Cingite, ne vati noceat mala lingua futuro,

The whole context is essential: the lines occur as Thyrsis opens
his answer in the singing match with Corydon, *Arcades ambo:*

Bring ivy-leaves to decorate your rising poet, shepherds of
Arcady, and so make Codrus burst his sides with envy. Or, if
he tries to harm me with excessive praise, twine foxglove round
my brows, to stop his evil tongue from hurting your predestined bard.[5]

That epigraph, summoning up the world of Vergil's *Eclogues,*

---

[5] In the translation of the *Eclogues* by E. V. Rieu (Penguin Books, London,
1949; Latin text included in third impression, 1954). Other translations here
from the *Eclogues* are also by Rieu. My quotations from the Latin text are given
according to Vergil's *Opera,* ed. F. A. Hirtzel (Oxford, 1900).

prepares the way for the many Vergilian characters and scenes to be encountered in the English poems here: Corydon and Thyrsis, Phillis and Thestylis, in *L'Allegro;* Thyrsis and Meliboeus in the *Mask*; Lycidas, Amaryllis, and Damoetas, with the setting of Vergil's seventh eclogue, "where the Mincius embroiders his banks with a green fringe of bending rushes"; and the shepherds of the Arcadian Entertainment at Harefield. The epigraph prepares us too for the echoes of Vergil's Messianic eclogue that occur in the volume's opening poem, the Nativity Ode; and, above all, it prepares us to watch, as we read the Latin poems, the poet's growth away from the light elegy toward the Vergilian mode in which Milton wrote the most mature and the finest of all the Latin verses in this volume: *Ad Patrem, Mansus,* and *Epitaphium Damonis,* all three of which confirm the "rising poet's" place as a "predestined bard."

In particular, the *Epitaphium Damonis,* spoken by Thyrsis, becomes appropriately the final poem of the entire volume, for with all its echoes of Greek pastoral it is the most deliberately Vergilian poem in the book. Here, clustered together, are those pastoral names that Vergil drew together in his *Eclogues:* Thyrsis and Damon, Daphnis, Tityrus, Alphesiboeus, Aegon, Amyntas, Mopsus, Aegle, and Menalcas; the use of the refrain reminds us of Vergil's eighth eclogue, the singing match between Damon and Alphesiboeus, while the words of Milton's refrain are modeled upon a line from the seventh eclogue (7.44) and also upon the final line of the last eclogue; the account of the two cups which Manso gave the poet is bound to recall the pairs of cups carved by Alcimedon, as described in Vergil's third eclogue;

and verbal echoes of Vergil are so frequent that the poem seems
to grow within a Vergilian matrix.[6]

The unity of Milton's volume, from title page to final poem,
is further suggested by the fact that the *Epitaphium Damonis*
laments the death of the very friend to whom the first Latin
poem in the book had been written—*Elegia prima,* that gay and
thoroughly Ovidian elegy composed by the arrogantly clever and
quite unrepentant sophomore during his rustication. At the same
time, the reader is bound to recall that *Elegia sexta* and the
fourth sonnet have also been explicitly addressed to this same
friend, Charles Diodati. The final poem, then, in paying tribute
to a friend of youth, becomes a farewell to the pleasures and
attitudes of youth, including the pleasures of pastoral poetry and
the imitative pleasures of writing such Latin verse—a farewell that Milton appropriately gives with unmistakable echoes
of Vergil's *Eclogues:*

> And I—for I know not what my pipe was grandly sounding—it
> is now eleven nights and a day—and then perhaps I had put my
> lips to new pipes, but they burst asunder, broken at the fasten-
> ing, and could no more bear the deep tones—I hesitate too
> lest I seem puffed up, yet I will tell the tale—give place then,
> O forests.[7]

Milton's *vos cedite silvae* is a clear echo of the *concedite silvae*
with which Gallus bids farewell to Arcadian pleasures in Vergil's

---

[6] The verbal echoes are explicit, not only from the *Eclogues,* but also from
the *Georgics* and the *Aeneid:* see MacKellar's admirable notes to this poem.

[7] This and the following translation are from MacKellar, ed., *Latin Poems,*
p. 169.

last eclogue (10.63); while Milton's following farewell to Latin poetry and Latin themes is based explicitly on the wording of Vergil's seventh eclogue:

> aut, si non possumus omnes,
>   hic arguta sacra pendebit fistula pinu.   (7.23–24)

Thus, after the famous passage in which Milton tells of his resolve to write an epic on British themes, he cries:

> O mihi tum si vita supersit,
> Tu procul annosa pendebis fistula pinu
> Multùm oblita mihi, aut patriis mutata camoenis
> Brittonicum strides, quid enim? omnia non licet uni
> Non sperasse uni licet omnia.

Ah! then if life remain, you, my pipe, shall hang on some aged pine far off and forgotten, unless forsaking your native songs you shrilly sound a British theme. Why not a British theme? One man cannot do all things, cannot hope to do all things.

MacKellar's version of these lines helps to bring out the complexity of the state of mind here expressed. The poet is resolved to leave behind the *fistula,* the reed pipe of his pastoral muse, and he will turn instead to write of those deeper themes which have already on one occasion proved to be stronger than that youthful pipe could bear. At the same time the *fistula* may represent Latin poetry, as MacKellar argues (p. 347), and the *patriis camoenis* may thus suggest the Latin language itself. That is to say, the poet is contemplating deeper themes, British themes,

and themes composed in English. The power of poetry represented by these early compositions on the *fistula* will not be
developed unless the poet can commit himself to English. Perhaps
he has already tried those deeper themes in Latin, but without
success: the rising poet knows, as Vergil says in the eighth
eclogue, *non omnia possumus omnes* (8.63); and he foresees
that his future fame must be entrusted to his native tongue.

The *Epitaphium* thus marks the end of an era that the whole
volume serves to celebrate and commemorate, while the whole
volume has been arranged to convey a sense of the predestined
bard's rising powers.

2

In two important studies W. R. Parker has shown how, within
carefully arranged groupings, the poems of this volume tend to
follow the chronological order of their composition.[8] This is
particularly clear in the Latin poems, most of which, as the
Latin title page points out, were written *intra Annum aetatis
Vigesimum:* that is, before his twentieth year had ended. In
keeping with this emphasis, Milton has taken unusual care in
dating his Latin poems, so as to make clear their youthfulness
and the rising poet's precociousness. This atmosphere is borne
out, in the elegies, by their heading *Liber primus*—a first book,
a primer, for which no second book follows; and also by the

---

[8] William Riley Parker, "Some Problems in the Chronology of Milton's Early
Poems," *Review of English Studies,* XI (1935), 276–83, and "Notes on the
Chronology of Milton's Latin Poems," in *A Tribute to George Coffin Taylor*
(Chapel Hill, N.C., 1952), pp. 113–31.

retractation which ends the sequence of the seven numbered elegies. There is no need to suspect a misprint in the dating of the seventh, which comes out of chronological order, for the placing of this elegy seems to be dictated by the presence of the retractation, evidently written for the seventh elegy alone, and not for this whole set of elegies; yet placed here as it is, the retractation covers any similar materials in the preceding poems and puts last the latest piece of composition, the retractation itself. This palinode creates the impression of having been composed for some special occasion (such as, perhaps, a recitation of the seventh elegy before one of those "privat Academies in *Italy*," where Milton tells us that he presented "some trifles . . . compos'd at under twenty or thereabout"),[9] when it was appropriate for the poet to speak of this youthful love poem with a tone of humorous exaggeration and a touch of mock-heroic banter:

These are the monuments to my wantonness that with a perverse spirit and a trifling purpose I once erected. Obviously, mischievous error led me astray and my undisciplined youth was a vicious teacher until the shady Academy offered its Socratic streams and taught me how to escape from the yoke to which I had submitted. From that hour those flames were extinct and thenceforward my breast has been rigid under a thick case of ice, of which the boy himself fears the frost for his arrows, and Venus herself is afraid of my Diomedean strength.[10]

[9] See *The Reason of Church-government*, prologue to Book 2, in *Complete Prose Works of John Milton*, ed. Don M. Wolfe (New Haven, 1953—), I, 809.
[10] Hughes, ed., *John Milton*, p. 61.

When we turn to the English poems, we find the dating less explicit in most cases, but the mode of arrangement equally clear. The group headed "Sonnets," for example, opens with the English love sonnet that echoes Italian addresses to the Nightingale, but basically follows the medieval and pseudo-Chaucerian tradition of the Cuckoo and the Nightingale. Then follow the five sonnets in Italian, with their *Canzone,* paying tribute to the Petrarchans by using, as Milton says, "the language of which Love makes his boast." [11] These are all poems written in the youthful atmosphere suggested by the opening line of Sonnet VI ("Giovane piano, e semplicetto amante"), and dramatized in the *Canzone,* where the poet shows himself surrounded by "Amorous young men and maidens . . . jesting." [12] After these playful exercises in a fading, once-popular mode, the stern lines on the flight of his three-and-twentieth year come with the shock of a sudden recognition, setting a severe Calvinist view of life against these early trifles:

> All is, if I have grace to use it so,
> As ever in my great task Masters eye.

The meaning of these much-discussed lines, I think, is clarified if we take the word "grace" in a strict Calvinist sense: the speaker's future lies completely in the hands of God. Though Time has stolen away his youth, all his hopes remain as valid as they ever were; nothing has really changed, for the use of his life depends upon the timeless will and eye and grace of God.

[11] From the last line of the *Canzone:* "Questa è lingua di cui si vanta Amore." *Ibid.,* p. 55.
[12] *Ibid.,* p. 54.

Nothing could form a sharper contrast with the preceding sonnets; and yet the sternness of the doctrine itself may suggest a
veering from one youthful extreme to another—especially since
the movement of the sonnet still maintains a conventional, end-
stopped, balanced manner. The succeeding sonnet on the military
threat to London shows, as we have seen, a greater maturity,
reflected in the graceful sentence that winds its sinewy length
over the last five lines.

Then the group closes with two more sonnets addressed to
women, both sonnets forming a tacit contrast with the Petrarchan mode, in theme and in technique. Recalling the "Donna"
of Milton's Italian sonnets, we are alert to appreciate the growth
and change represented in the strongly suspended opening of
Sonnet IX:

> Lady that in the prime of earliest youth,
>> Wisely hast shun'd the broad way and the green,
>> And with those few art eminently seen,
>> That labour up the Hill of heav'nly Truth,
> The better part with *Mary,* and [with] *Ruth,*
>> Chosen thou hast. . .

Lastly, Sonnet X, with an even greater suspension and involu-
tion, addresses a married lady who in herself maintains the
virtues that once ruled in England, before the turmoil of the
present age began:

> Daughter to that good Earl, once President
> Of *Englands* Counsel, and her Treasury,

Who liv'd in both, unstain'd with gold or fee,
    And left them both, more in himself content,
Till the sad breaking of that Parlament
    Broke him, as that dishonest victory
    At *Chaeronéa,* fatal to liberty
    Kil'd with report that Old man eloquent,
Though later born, then to have known the dayes
    Wherin your Father flourisht, yet by you
    Madam, me thinks I see him living yet;
So well your words his noble vertues praise,
    That all both judge you to relate them true,
    And to possess them, Honour'd *Margaret.*

Thus the syntax involves the troubled, more inclusive vision of maturity, while the *disio amoroso* of the Italian sonnets lies far in the past.

Similarly, it is helpful to read *L'Allegro* and *Il Penseroso* in the context of Milton's chosen arrangement; for these two poems come at the end of a group that might best be described as Jonsonian: poems in the mode of the "terse" couplet characteristic of Jonson and his Sons. First, the "witty" *Epitaph on the Marchioness of Winchester;* next, that perfect distillation of the Elizabethan madrigal, the *Song On May morning;* then the rather labored epigram on Shakespeare, dated 1630, and marked as early by the archaic "Star-ypointing"; and then the two jocular epitaphs for the University Carrier. Out of these experiments arise the two great companion poems, or twin poems, or the double poem, as we have come to call them. Reading these two poems in their original context may guide us toward a slight modification or qualification of these descriptive phrases. They are companion poems, certainly, but, as Don Cameron Allen has contended, they are not of equal strength and stature.[13] Their relation is rather that of Younger Brother to Elder Brother. The parallels between them, so familar to everyone, should not lead us to read the poems in parallel, as though they were two sides of a coin, or two sides of an academic debate. For the poems develop a linear, sequential effect, moving from youthful hedonism toward the philosophic, contemplative mind.[14]

L'Allegro's dismissal of "loathed Melancholy" is extreme and violent, too violent to be taken seriously; while Il Penseroso's dismissal of "vain deluding joyes" is by comparison thoroughly under control, judicious, and temperate. The first poem sums up a youthful Elizabethan world of poetry now past: the tone is set by the opening archaism, "In Heav'n ycleap'd *Euphrosyne.*" It is full of all the maying and the pastoral joys celebrated in hundreds of Elizabethan songs and madrigals, including the famous "Come live with me," strongly echoed near the beginning (l. 39) and at the end; and it remembers too those popular legends about Mab and the drudging Goblin, celebrated by Shakespeare and Drayton. One notes that, in Leishman's fine study of the literary echoes in these poems, most of the parallels with Elizabethan, Shakespearean, and seventeenth-century poetry

---

[13] See D. C. Allen's essay on these poems in *The Harmonious Vision* (Baltimore, 1954), pp. 3–23.

[14] See the important brief essay by Kester Svendsen in *Explicator,* Vol. VIII (May, 1950), Item 49; here Svendsen deals with "the dynamics of the twin poem," showing "the progressive emphasis in both parts on images of sound and music." He notes how, in the finale of *Il Penseroso,* "the many references to sound and in particular to music build toward this conclusion, so that structurally it is the end of a progressive development within both poems."

are found in *L'Allegro*.[15] Then there are the overt allusions to
the "high triumphs" of archaic chivalry, to the courtly "Ladies,
whose bright eies/ Rain influence" in Petrarchan fashion, to
"mask, and antique Pageantry," to Jonson's comedies, and to
Shakespeare in his comic and pastoral vein. It is a joyous celebration and re-creation of an era, a state of mind, now past; but
we note that it ends with hints of imperfection in this mode of
harmony. As every Platonist knew, Plato had condemned the
"soft *Lydian* Aires," and Milton subtly recalls the condemnation,
while seeming to ignore it:

> With wanton heed, and giddy cunning,
> The melting voice through mazes running;
> Untwisting all the chains that ty
> The hidden soul of harmony.

But the words "wanton," "giddy," and "melting" recall the
implications of the *Republic*:

> Again, drunkenness, effeminacy, and inactivity are most
> unsuitable in Guardians. Which are the modes expressing
> softness and the ones used at drinking-parties?
>
> There are the Ionian and certain Lydian modes which are
> called "slack."
>
> You will not use them in the training of your warriors?
> Certainly not.[16]

---

[15] J. B. Leishman, *"L'Allegro* and *Il Penseroso* in Their Relation to Seventeenth-
Century Poetry," *Essays and Studies,* N.S., IV (1951), 1–36.

[16] *Republic,* III.398c–400c; in the translation by F. M. Cornford (New York,
1945), pp. 86–87.

And does one really produce harmony by untwisting *all* the chains that tie? The final picture of Orpheus heaving up his head "From golden slumber on a bed/ Of heapt *Elysian* flowres" carries on, however beautifully, the "softness" of the Lydian mode. We note, by contrast, how the second poem invokes Orpheus in a potent, active role, singing

> Such notes as warbled to the string,
> Drew Iron tears down *Pluto's* cheek,
> And made Hell grant what Love did seek.

Furthermore, this second reference to Orpheus is subsumed within the middle of *Il Penseroso,* where he is only one of many great poets and thinkers: Hermes, Plato, the Greek tragedians, Musaeus, Chaucer, Spenser. The spirit of Plato's "shady Academy" dominates *Il Penseroso,* from the opening salutation of the Goddess "sage and holy" to the grand musical close which extends this poem two dozen lines beyond the length of *L'Allegro,* to present a movement toward the "extasies" of Neoplatonic mysticism. All is, however, moderated and controlled by the quiet, detached tone of the poet, as at the very end he presents a picture that is too obviously archaic and sentimental to be taken solemnly: its excess tells us that Melancholy too needs tempering:

> And may at last my weary age
> Find out the peacefull hermitage,
> The Hairy Gown and Mossy Cell,
> Where I may sit and rightly spell,
> Of every Star that Heav'n doth shew,

> And every Herb that sips the dew;
> Till old experience do attain
> To something like Prophetic strain.
> These pleasures *Melancholy* give,
> And I with thee will choose to live.

That echo of "Come live with me" is phrased more positively than the closing couplet of *L'Allegro:*

> These delights, if thou canst give,
> Mirth with thee, I mean to live.

Yet the echo reminds us that either choice involves a limitation.

Thus the two poems move from youth to age—the word "youthfull" is invoked twice in *L'Allegro,* and not at all in *Il Penseroso*—while in their movement these two unequal but compatible companions suggest the growth toward maturity that constitutes this volume's dominant theme.

3

Beyond the developments observable within these various subgroupings, each part of the volume displays a larger movement. As the Latin part begins with a youthful elegy and ends with a farewell to youth, so the English part begins with poems of youth and ends with *Lycidas* and the Ludlow *Mask:* two poems that in themselves enact a movement toward the broader visions of maturity. The essays following will, I think, suggest the integral relation of these two great poems to the dominant theme implied by Milton's arrangement of his volume. Here, by way of prelude and conclusion, I should like to consider the ways in which the development of this central theme is foreshadowed in the group of religious poems that Milton has chosen to open his volume of 1645.

Milton has carefully stressed the youthfulness of the four opening poems. First, out of strict chronological order, we have the poem headed: *On the morning of Christs Nativity. Compos'd 1629.*—with the date thus given prominence as part of the title. Then come the two Psalms, "don by the Author at fifteen years old," as the headnote tells us. Then the unfinished poem on the Passion, with the famous note at the end: "This Subject the Author finding to be above the yeers he had, when he wrote it, and nothing satisfi'd with what was begun, left it unfinisht." One may wonder why Milton bothered to include this acknowledged failure and fragment, when he did not include the more interesting and at least completed English poems that he added in 1673: the poem *On the Death of a fair Infant,* and the lines from the Vacation Exercise. But the inclusion of the fragment has a clear function: to stress the immaturity of these opening pieces, to suggest the ambitious young man outreaching his powers, and achieving poetical success only when he can subject his muse to some deliberate limitation. What he can accomplish is then demonstrated in the three short pieces that follow: *On Time, Upon the Circumcision,* and *At a solemn Musick;* these are undated, and thus, we assume, not quite so youthful. *Upon the Circumcision,* in particular, suggests a new beginning, in a less venturous mode, after the false start of *The Passion;* here the poet creates, within two madrigal-like stanzas, a carefully designed and reasoned meditation on the love of the suffering

Infant. The other two lyrics are experiments in the handling of the canzone, anticipating the flexible verse form of *Lycidas*.

But all these brief experiments are insignificant when set beside the remarkable success of the long poem which is rightly placed first, as prologue to the rising poet's achievement. Its dating, "Compos'd 1629," accords with the poem's relation to an age and mode of English poetry now outgrown, both by the nation and by the poet. In understanding this poetical mode, one may gain important clues from Milton's description of the Nativity Ode in his sixth Latin elegy—especially when we read this elegy in Milton's chosen context, between the pagan celebration of Spring in Elegy Five and the mildly Ovidian eroticism of Elegy Seven. Read thus, Elegy Six does not lend itself easily to the widely held interpretation expressed, for example, by Woodhouse:

> The Ode teaches us to read the contrast of the elegiac and the heroic vein as a repudiation of the former, to transliterate the description of the heroic poet into Christian terms as the account of a dedicated spirit divinely inspired, and to see in the ascetic discipline referred to, a turning towards that moral and religious preparation for his life-work on which Milton finally entered at Horton.[17]

---

[17] A. S. P. Woodhouse, "Notes on Milton's Early Development," *University of Toronto Quarterly*, XIII (1943), 66–101; see p. 75. W. R. Parker, in a review (*Modern Language Notes*, LV [1940], 216–17), has strongly disagreed with this interpretation of Elegy Six as given by E. M. W. Tillyard in *The Miltonic Setting* (Cambridge, 1938); see, for example, p. 179 of Tillyard's book: "The neophytic and ascetic tone of *Elegia Sexta* fits well enough with his self-dedication to heroic poetry."

This elegy begins with a broad joke about Diodati's feasting at the Christmas season: "With a stomach anything but full, I send you a prayer for sound health, of which, perhaps, you, with your stomach stretched to its uttermost, may be in sore need." [18] Then follows lively praise of the "light elegy," in a passage twice as long as the subsequent praise of epic: wine, feasting, maidens, and dancing inspire, says Milton, an excellent kind of poetry, blessed by many gods. Of course, he adds, if a poet wants to write on grand epic themes, then he must live quite differently; and Milton proceeds to write a hyperbolical account of the ascetic life required for such a bard: "let herbs furnish his innocent diet. Let the purest water stand beside him in a bowl of beech and let him drink sober draughts from the pure spring." He goes on to express his belief in the exalted power of this kind of bard, but he does not wholly lay aside the tone of "Ovidian banter" that Rand has found in the earlier part.[19] Milton no doubt hopes to reach that higher vein himself; but he does not appear to be saying so here. When he turns to discuss himself at the end of the poem, he makes a clean break with the previous discussion of elegy and epic; both are excellent in their kinds, the poet implies, but he is not writing in either vein at the moment. One must stress the *At tu si quid agam, scitabere:* "But if you will know what I am doing (if only you think it of any importance to know whether I am doing anything)"—note how

---

[18] From the translation by Charles Knapp in the Columbia edition of *The Works of John Milton* (New York, 1931–38), I, 207. The other passages translated from this poem are taken from Hughes, ed., *John Milton,* pp. 52–53.

[19] E. K. Rand, "Milton in Rustication," *Studies in Philology,* XIX (1922), 109–35; see pages 110, 124.

he maintains the familiar tone with which the poem has opened—
"I am singing the heaven-descended King, the bringer of peace,
and the blessed times promised in the sacred books—the infant
cries of our God" [which in fact are not mentioned in the Nativity poem as we have it; but Milton is emphasizing the poem's
allegiance to the naïve tradition of the Christmas carol, as his
next words further indicate] "and his stabling under a mean roof
who, with his Father, governs the realms above. I am singing
the starry sky and the hosts that sang high in air, and the gods
that were suddenly destroyed in their own shrines. These are
my gifts for the birthday of Christ—gifts which the first light
of its dawn brought to me." In that last clause Milton seems to
be saying only that the thought of writing such a poem came to
him at dawn; there seems to be no indication of some special
experience of religious conversion.

In this elegy's final couplet the opening *Te quoque* has allowed
various interpretations:

> Te quoque pressa manent patriis meditata cicutis,
> Tu mihi, cui recitem, judicis instar eris.

In some versions (as in that of the Columbia edition) it appears
that Milton is referring to certain *other* English poems that he
has also written; but the *quoque* modifies *te;* or, rather, it is
pleonastic and is best omitted, as in the revised translation of
Hughes, which makes it plain that the passage is still alluding
to the Nativity poem: "For you these simple strains that have
been meditated on my native pipes are waiting; and you, when
I recite them to you, shall be my judge." *Patriis meditata cicutis:*

meditated on the native hemlock pipes of the humble shepherd. Milton has suggested here the poem's basic decorum.

It is, first of all, a poem that declares, in many ways, this poet's indebtedness to his predecessors in the line of English poetry. The four prefatory stanzas, written in a variation of rhyme royal, suggest the use of this ancient stanza form by Chaucer and the Chaucerians, by Spenser, in *The Ruines of Time* and the *Fowre Hymnes,* and by Shakespeare, in *Lucrece;* while the modification into hexameter in the final line declares a further allegiance to Spenser and the Spenserians. The stanza of the Hymn proper is even more significant, for its first six lines suggest the movement of a popular song or carol:

> It was the Winter wilde,
> While the Heav'n-born-childe,
> >   All meanly wrapt in the rude manger lies;
> Nature in aw to him
> Had doff't her gawdy trim,
> >   With her great Master so to sympathize.

The use of three-foot and five-foot lines, in various combinations, is found in many Elizabethan songs: thus among Thomas Morley's canzonets we find this stanza running 335335335, though the rhyme differs from Milton's:

> I follow, lo, the footing
> Still of my lovely cruel,
> Proud of herself that she is beauty's jewel.
> >   And fast away she flieth,

Love's sweet delight deriding,
In woods and groves sweet Nature's treasure hiding.
Yet cease I not pursuing,
But since I thus have sought her,
Will run me out of breath till I have caught her.[20]

But the first six lines of Milton's stanza also suggest another pattern: the combination of two- and three-foot lines, with Milton's rhyme scheme, found in some of the ancient Christmas carols:

> The God Almyght
> And Kyng of Lyght,
>   Whose powr is ouer all,
> Gyue vs of grace
> For to purchas
>   Hys realme celestyall.
>
> Wher hys aungels
> And archangels
>   Do syng incessantly,
> Hys princypates
> And potestates
>   Maketh gret armony.
>
> The cherubyns
> And seraphyns
>   With ther tvnykes mery,

[20] *English Madrigal Verse, 1588–1632,* ed. E. H. Fellowes (2d ed., Oxford, 1929), p. 141.

> The trones al,
> Most musycall,
>   Syng the heuenly Kery.[21]

Then, by allowing his last line to swell out into a Spenserian Alexandrine, Milton draws his poem out of the realm of the popular song into the larger area of this poet's predestined goals. In stanza after stanza we may feel this change from the simple language and steady beat of the ballad into the realms of a more ambitious art:

> But wisest Fate sayes no,
> This must not yet be so,
>   The Babe lies yet in smiling Infancy,
> That on the bitter cross
> Must redeem our loss;
>   So both himself and us to glorifie:
> Yet first to those ychain'd in sleep,
> The wakefull trump of doom must thunder through the deep.

Yet with all the poem's lofty expansions in rhythm, in language, and in rich allusion, the poet's chosen method of control never falters: he clings to the central mode of the ancient naïve, the mode of the nativity ballad, the mode that Milton points to when he calls his poem a "humble ode" that he seeks to lay "lowly at his blessed feet." The touches of archaic, Spenserian language sprinkled throughout, very lightly, are all adjusted to maintain this effect, as in the "ychain'd" of the stanza just quoted, the

---

[21] *The Early English Carols,* ed. Richard Leighton Greene (Oxford, 1935), p. 58. I have omitted the editor's brackets and italics.

"lusty Paramour" of the Hymn's opening stanza, the "silly thoughts" of the shepherds, or the "dusky eyn" of the doomed god Osiris. At the same time touches of old-fashioned heavy alliteration recall the style, not only of Spenser, but of all those lesser writers whom Sidney mocked for their "rimes, running in ratling rowes."

This decorum of an ancient and traditional simplicity pervades every aspect of the poem, versification, language, scene painting, imagery, and theme. The scenes and images are given in broad and simplified terms, as in some old tapestry or pageant. The original line in which Truth and Justice wear "Th'enameld *Arras* of the Rainbow" is more closely in accord with the poem than Milton's more sophisticated revision: "Orb'd in a Rain-bow." Thus Nature seeks to hide her "guilty front" with "The Saintly Vail of Maiden white"; and "the meek-eyd Peace . . . crown'd with Olive green, came softly sliding/ Down through the turning sphear." "The Shepherds on the Lawn . . . Sate simply chatting in a rustick row"; then

> At last surrounds their sight
> A Globe of circular light,
>   That with long beams the shame-fac't night array'd,
> The helmed Cherubim
> And sworded Seraphim,
>   Are seen in glittering ranks with wings displaid.

One should note, too, in these quotations, the curious mixture of past and present tense, which Lowry Nelson has ably inter-

preted to indicate the poem's sense of a timeless world;[22] this is
so, yet Milton's manner of thus mixing past and present also
adds to the effect of the naïve, as though the poet were artlessly
following the instinct of a momentary mood or were using past
and present tense as the needs of rhythm and rhyme might, for
a moment, require.

Then, in the latter half of the poem, this effect is strongly
heightened by Milton's treatment of the various characters that
here are shown in action. The Dragon of Revelation is presented
in the guise of a dragon out of folklore:

> And wrath to see his Kingdom fail,
> Swindges the scaly Horrour of his foulded tail.

And his antagonist, the blessed Babe, is likewise shown in the
manner of some ancient folk-hero, some infant Hercules:

> Our Babe to shew his Godhead true,
> Can in his swadling bands controul the damned crew.

Meanwhile, in the superb rendition of the fall of the pagan
deities, it is helpful, while we recognize the foreshadowing of
Paradise Lost, to notice also how utterly lacking in sophistication
this account is, when compared with Milton's later roll call of
the fallen angels. In *Paradise Lost* it is made plain that these are
devils adored as deities, and the horror of the deception is brought
home by showing in detail the effect of these devils upon
mankind:

[22] Lowry Nelson, Jr., *Baroque Lyric Poetry* (New Haven, 1961), pp. 41–52.

> First *Moloch,* horrid King besmear'd with blood
> Of human sacrifice, and parents tears,
> Though for the noyse of Drums and Timbrels loud
> Their childrens cries unheard, that past through fire
> To his grim Idol. Him the *Ammonite*
> Worshipt in *Rabba* and her watry Plain,   (1.392–97)

and so on for eight more lines of particular detail, showing the ravages wrought by Moloch on the earth.

But here in the Nativity poem Moloch is simply mentioned as a totally defeated character, while the scene of his idolatry is represented in elementary colors and sounds:

> And sullen *Moloch* fled,
> Hath left in shadows dred,
>   His burning Idol all of blackest hue,
> In vain with Cymbals ring,
> They call the grisly king,
>   In dismall dance about the furnace blue.

These vanquished gods are not devils in disguise; they are the supernatural beings of antique folklore, who exist in their own right as a part of nature, a part of man's primitive consciousness of forces that lie beyond his control:

> The lonely mountains o're,
> And the resounding shore,
>   A voice of weeping heard, and loud lament;
> From haunted spring, and dale
> Edg'd with poplar pale,

> The parting Genius is with sighing sent,
> With flowre-inwov'n tresses torn
> The Nimphs in twilight shade of tangled thickets mourn.

Finally, bringing to a brilliant close this basic effect of the simple and naïve, Milton ends with two stanzas that sum up the basic techniques and attitudes of the poem. First we have the poem's most extravagantly naïve image—one that would have offended at the outset—but, now, with our minds attuned to the poem's peculiar decorum, we can perhaps accept it as a youthful excess:

> So when the Sun in bed,
> Curtain'd with cloudy red,
> Pillows his chin upon an Orient wave.

Then come the ghosts and fairies of folklore, treated with sympathy and even affection:

> The flocking shadows pale,
> Troop to th'infernall jail,
> Each fetter'd Ghost slips to his severall grave,
> And the yellow-skirted *Fayes,*
> Fly after the Night-steeds, leaving their Moon-lov'd maze.

And lastly, we return to the traditional scene, ten thousand times represented in ancient poetry and painting: the manger scene upon which this technique of the naïve has been based:

> But see the Virgin blest,
> Hath laid her Babe to rest.
> Time is our tedious Song should here have ending.

Here, still, is the simple, humble singer, who is well aware of his defects, but nevertheless has been led by gratitude to sing this song of praise:

> Heav'ns youngest teemed Star,
> Hath fixt her polisht Car,
>   Her sleeping Lord with Handmaid Lamp attending.

All Heaven, whether physical or spiritual, stands fixed in a service of unlabored elegance:

> And all about the Courtly Stable,
> Bright-harnest Angels sit in order serviceable.

The last rhyme seems to call attention to the way in which Milton has contrived, within his chosen mode, to make even the poem's defects appear as virtues, contributing to the total effect of the youthful singer writing as well as he can in an ancient, traditional manner of tribute. The poem is a total success because Milton has chosen and maintained a mode of writing that does not tempt him beyond the range of his precocious powers.

That is not to say that the poem is simple-minded in the range of its implications, but that the chosen mode of simplicity creates a world in which theological problems are pushed beyond the fringe of our vision; there is no sense of struggling with theological issues, no sense that we need to consult the church fathers, no sense of attempting to enforce anything but the most easily grasped and broadly acceptable truths. This, says the poet, is the happy morn when, as everyone knows,

> the Son of Heav'ns eternal King,
> Of wedded Maid, and Virgin Mother born,
> Our great redemption from above did bring.

Everyone shares the story, how the Son laid aside the majesty that was his due as part of Trinal Unity,

> and here with us to be,
> Forsook the Courts of everlasting Day,
> And chose with us a darksom House of mortal Clay.

How can we express our gratitude for this gift of the Almighty? By a song of praise for the peace and harmony that the divine child has brought to earth, not only on the day of his birth, and in the long-range future, but, in some measure, now: it "now begins," as this poet can best testify by writing a song that in itself represents a simple and unworried harmony.

But—"Compos'd 1629." More difficult and much more complex harmonies lie ahead for the rising poet, the predestined bard.

C. L. Barber

A MASK PRESENTED AT LUDLOW

CASTLE: THE MASQUE AS A MASQUE

Two questions have confronted me in reading Milton's Ludlow *Mask*. How does Milton succeed—and I feel he does succeed—in making a happy work which centers, seemingly, on the denial of impulse, when typically in the Renaissance such works involve, in some fashion or other, release from restraint? Second, what is the form of the piece? how does it relate to Renaissance comedy and allied traditions? The answer to the question about its form, with which I shall begin, will I hope provide means for understanding how it orders and satisfies feeling.

I. The Form of the Masque as a Noble Entertainment

The *work* of criticism, as against the pleasure, is in good part the altering of expectations to suit the thing in hand. My experience with *A Mask Presented at Ludlow Castle* has been a case in point: it has involved giving up expectations of drama for expectations appropriate to the masque. Invited to consider Milton's masque as comedy, I report back after six months that

Milton's masque is a masque! This shift in expectation has permitted me, I think, to get past difficulties which were fundamentally the same as those which Johnson expressed with his usual candor. "A work more truly poetical is rarely found," he said, but went on to object that it is not dramatic:

> The discourse of the Spirit is too long—an objection that may be made to almost all of the following speeches; they have not the sprightliness of a dialogue animated by reciprocal contention, but seem rather declamations deliberately composed, and formally repeated, on a moral question. The auditor therefore listens to a lecture, without passion, without anxiety.
>
> . . . At last the Brothers enter, with too much tranquility; and when they have feared lest their sister should be in danger, and hoped she is not in danger, the Elder makes a speech in praise of chastity, and the Younger finds how fine it is to be a philosopher.
>
> Then descends the Spirit in the form of a shepherd, and the Brother, instead of being in haste to ask his help, praises his singing, and inquires his business in that place. It is remarkable, that at this interview the Brother is taken with a short fit of rhyming. The Spirit relates that the Lady is in the power of Comus; the brother moralises again; and the Spirit makes a long narration, of no use because it is false, and therefore unsuitable for a good being.[1]

I decided to quote Johnson when it struck me that his mocking summary of the plot is just like the fun people make of operas

[1] *Live of the English Poets* (Everyman's Library; New York, n.d.), pp. 98–99.

when they do not understand how opera works, or are sick of it. All they have to do is recite the plot. "The Brother, instead of being in haste to ask [the shepherd's] help, praises his singing. . . . It is remarkable, that at this interview the Brother is taken with a short fit of rhyming." It is indeed remarkable—the rhyme has a formal, musical function to which Johnson is turning a deaf ear:

> *2 Bro.* O brother, 'tis my father's shepherd sure.
> *El. Bro.* Thyrsis? Whose artful strains have oft delaid
> The huddling brook to hear his madrigal,
> And sweeten'd every muskrose of the dale,
> How cam'st thou here good swain? hath any ram
> Slip't from the fold, or young kid lost his dam? [2]

Mr. Hardy, in the Brooks and Hardy study, finds this moment of recognition "one of exquisite dramatic irony," and goes after the Elder Brother, who he says "greets his father's hired man with easy condescention," while ironically "the Spirit plays his assumed role dutifully." [3] Throughout his elaborate treatment, Mr. Hardy is intent on finding dramatic irony between or behind the lines. His assumption is that, to save the piece from being silly or flat in the way that Johnson thought it, we must find character, drama, irony. There *is* irony and drama in it, certainly. But these are not what makes it work as a whole, as I see it; it works as

---

[2] Quotations are from *Milton's Poems 1645* (Type-facsimile; Oxford, 1924). I have corrected obvious misprints, such as the omission of the possessive in the first line here, which reads "my father Shepherd"; and I have omitted the capitalized first letters of such words as "shepherd."

[3] *Poems of Mr. John Milton: The 1645 Edition with Essays in Analysis*, by Cleanth Brooks and John Edward Hardy (New York, 1951), p. 209.

a whole as a masque. So in the greeting of the Elder Brother to Thyrsis, it seems to me that Mr. Hardy sees a kind of action that isn't there, ignoring the action that is taking place. What is taking place is the creation and relishing of a pastoral setting, by means of a poetry of heightened formal lyricism. The Brother's question serves to set moving in the direction of the lost lady the conventional pastoral metaphor of the strayed sheep; Thyrsis develops it by antithesis:

> I came not here on such a trivial toy
> As a stray'd ewe . . .
>
> .   .   .
>
> But O my virgin Lady, where is she?

Dr. Johnson's high praise of the masque's poetry "as a series of lines" combines strangely with his complaint that almost all the speeches are too long—" 'Tis a very excellent piece of work, madam lady: would 'twere done!"

To consider how the masque form operates, let me begin by laying out what is almost self-evident. As drama is shaped by its changing environment, the theater, so the masque form was shaped by its extinct environment, the noble entertainment. The masque, indeed, is only one specialized form of a whole species of entertainment literature or pastime. The basic function of it all was to contribute meaning and beauty to noble persons, noble places, noble occasions. A masque was *presented,* not performed. Its basic method was to extend actuality by fiction, fictions developed out of the circumstances of the occasion and pointing back to realities. At its best, the make-believe was not merely added; it served to find or express meaning which was already essentially present, or ideally might be, should be, present. When Elizabeth visited a noble household, a distressed nymph from Ovid might rive an oak and implore the aid of Diana—in actuality Elizabeth was quite a fierce Diana in governing her ladies in waiting. The idealization tended to become flattery; the elaboration merely decorative. But the masquing could also be revelatory, exemplary, and persuasive, inviting nobility to realize an ideal in miming it.

The action common to almost all entertainments is greeting or encountering, with explanation which describes the occasion of the meeting so as to redefine the place and persons in terms of pastoral mythology and local lore. Visits or embassages were such fine opportunities that the formal court masque developed as a way of arranging for a visit where no actual visit was involved. The masquers tell of their origins and of their journey to the magnetic royal presence, present themselves in dance, are greeted in dance by undisguised lords or ladies, make their obeisance, and depart. In the Jacobean court, Inigo Jones's settings made visible the fabulous places from which and through which the visitors came. The masque became a way of environing a court ball, or "revel," with the pleasures of light opera and ballet. Jonson brought in the antimasque at court, drawing on the tradition at country entertainments of presenting pastimes of the common folk and on the satirical burlesque of the popular stage. The antimasquers are visitors too, or intruders, common and grotesque; they were usually played by professional entertainers who were proof against the obloquy of such miming, and skilled for it; the noble participants mimed beauty, virtue, deity, and the like, which is easy if one has the clothes. Their real skill, and it was a skill, was in dancing.

So majesty visited itself to realize majesty. The court masque was only possible so long as there was majesty to realize, or, in the great households, nobility. If James as a person was scarcely majestic, Jonson and Jones could make him so. Indeed the Stuart elaboration of the masque can be regarded as a compensation: Elizabeth would not have needed it all, and certainly would not have paid for it all! Under James, as Miss Welsford's fine book shows,[4] the masque was an important if precarious means of upholding the sense of a collective life consummated in magnificence at court—even while outside its charmed circle powerful elements in society were finding it irrelevant, or worse.

During the uneasy Caroline calm, Milton was, fortunately, enough a man of the age to enjoy the virtues of aristocratic courtesy and the courteous art of the masque. But, of course, he also felt responsible to a wider frame. In *Arcades* he wrote "part of an entertainment presented to the Countess Dowager of Darby at Harefield."

> Look, nymphs, and shepherds, look,
> What sudden blaze of majesty
> Is that which we from hence descry
> Too divine to be mistook:
>   This this is she
> To whom our vows and wishes bend,
> Heer our solemn search hath end.

[4] Enid Welsford, *The Court Masque: A Study in the Relationship between Poetry and the Revels* (Cambridge, 1927), especially Part Three.

The Presenter, the Genius of the Wood, explains that the masquers have come from "famous Arcady" and arrived at a still better place: "Such a rural queen/ All Arcadia hath not seen." This simple redefinition of Harefield and its household is perfectly conventional and perfectly done: Milton does not withhold himself from compliment.

But the speech of the Genius contains lines which describe a setting beyond Arcady:

> in deep of night when drowsines
> Hath lockt up mortal sense, then listen I
> To the celestial Sirens' harmony,
> That sit upon the nine enfolded sphears,
> And sing to those that hold the vital shears,
> And turn the adamantine spindle round,
> On which the fate of gods and men is wound.

Milton's mind flies up beyond festive song to a permanent music, sublimely Orphic.

> Such sweet compulsion doth in musick ly,
> To lull the daughters of necessity,
> And keep unsteady nature to her law,
> And the low world in measur'd motion draw
> After the heavenly tune, which none can hear
> Of human mould with grosse unpurged ear.

What can be the relevance of such music at a great household's entertainment? At a religious concert or in church, "at a solemn music," sacred music imitates divine, as Milton's poem about such an occasion beautifully says, marking as it does so the sad jar of sin that comes between. Here in *Arcades* all he can do with the music of the spheres is use it in compliment. If we *could* hear it, the Genius says,

> such musick worthiest were to blaze
> The peerless height of her immortal praise,
> Whose lustre leads us, and for her most fit,
> If my inferior hand or voice could hit
> Inimitable sounds . . .

If we pause over this transition, we can feel the difficulty involved in the masque form as a vehicle for Milton's full sensibility. For would such music really be appropriate "to blaze/ The peerless height of [the] immortal praise" of the Dowager Countess of Derby, however sublimed? The word "immortal," when we pause over the use of it in compliment, wavers unsteadily under the weight of the previous immense conception.

II. Milton's Strategy in Using the Masque Form

At Ludlow, Milton did, astonishingly enough, convert the masque to his high purposes. His second masque leaves out all but a decent measure of compliment, converting the approach to the presence, normally a climax of adulation, into a family reunion, with children honoring parents. There was an element of this already at Harefield, where members of the Duchess' family were the masquers. There was doubtless at Harefield an account of their journey to her presence: "Here our solemn search hath end." Milton either did not write that part or did not preserve it—there is nothing in the finale to indicate what sort of difficulties the journey involved. At Ludlow the journey becomes central. One side of our interest is centered in the trial of the Lady in her passage through a Spenserian dark wood. The leading masquer becomes a dramatic protagonist, and the spokesman for the antimasque becomes an antagonist, a vile enchanter who, so far as his attributes are concerned, might have stepped out from the pages of *The Faerie Queene.*

It is often assumed that, in making a drama centering on the Lady, Milton leaves the masque form behind. But this drama develops by the masque's kind of unfolding of the situation in which the drama takes place. And this situation is not simple fiction, as in drama, but rather transformation or translation of the actual, in keeping with the masque form and occasion. Milton was familiar with dramatic works which present a self-contained action shaped by traditions of the noble entertainment, notably *A Midsummer Night's Dream* and *The Tempest,* probably also Fletcher's relatively trivial teen-age pastoral romp, *The Faithful Shepherdess.* Shakespeare's habits as a professional dramatist, and his natural concern to add to the repertory of his company, led him to produce entertainments which could be reused as public stage plays. Milton, working with Henry Lawes at his elbow, for Lawes's patron, had no such further theatrical purpose. When Lawes in 1637 published *A Maske Presented at Ludlow Castle, 1634: On Michaelmasse Night, before the Right Honorable John Earle of Bridgewater,* etc., the title and the dedication invite the reader to share in retrospect the occasion of its presentation. So, in reading, we must reanimate not only the work's fictions but also the literal circumstances which those fictions extended.

To look at what was regularly being done with the masque's resources for transforming or redefining the situation at an entertainment makes one realize what an emphatic thing Milton did with it. In *Coelum Britannicum,* performed on Shrove Tuesday of the same year as Milton's masque, Thomas Carew and Inigo Jones undertook to transform Charles and his chaste court into the stars of heaven, replacing the lewd constellations with which the sky had been cluttered by Jove's lusts![5] The Edgerton brothers played the part of lesser stars, torchbearers to the masquers. The animal heads used at Ludlow for Comus' rout may well have been the same which served at court for a dance of bestial constellations, on their way to oblivion. *Coelum Brittanicum* was clearly a very successful occasion. The thing worked by combining a light touch about the mythology with truly effective spectacle, song, and dance—a combination very like that which brings off our better musical comedies. To be subjected to Inigo Jones's settings must have been rather like the 3-D experience of cinerama: for Carew's masque, lights on a great globe of the heavens progressively went out, later to come

---

[5] *The Poems of Thomas Carew, with His Masque "Coelum Britannicum,"* ed. Rhodes Dunlap (Oxford, 1949), p. 183. The masque was presented by the king to the queen in return for a Twelfth Night performance of *The Faithful Shepherdess*. Dunlap quotes from a letter of Garrard to Stafford: "There are two Masques in Hand, . . . High Expences . . . Oh that they would once give over these Things, or lay them aside for a Time, and bend all their Endeavours to make the King Rich! For it gives me no Satisfaction, who am but a looker on, to see a rich Commonwealth, a rich People, and the Crown poor. God direct them to remedy this quickly" (p. 273). Sir Henry Herbert, however, recorded his satisfaction that "the Q. was pleased to tell mee before the king, 'Pour les habits, elle n'avoit jamais rien vue de si brave' " (*ibid.*).

on again in a blaze, "expressing the stellifying of our British Heroes." In the interval, a huge mountain rose; clouds caromed, with singers on them. Another of Jones's great resources, not used in this particular masque, was the sudden opening up of vista beyond vista. His goal was not simply to present a scene but to alter the situation of the observer by manipulating perspective, as baroque painters sought to do when, for example, they painted domes to make the observer seem to look straight up a column of air in which angels were descending, some high, others almost on top of him.

What Milton did in his Ludlow masque was to use the masque's altering and extending of situation with his own kind of seriousness. The form sanctioned reaching out to far and high things, "stellifying." As Professor William R. Parker points out,[6] Milton and posterity benefited from the fact that at Ludlow physical scenery was necessarily minimal; this was to be a masque where poetry, rather than Inigo Jones, would present the descents from above and open out the vistas. Milton did not use directly Christian iconography in redefining the entertainment situation as a Christian situation. To have done so would have been discourteous, indecorous in a social sense. In the masque form there was no distinction between social decorum and artistic decorum. Mr. Martz's essay brings out how, in the 1645 volume as a whole, Milton's concern with decorum is social, the conscious development of roles or attitudes of the poet in society. A masque was an occasion for "antique fables" and "fairy toys," classical mythology and native folklore; Milton accordingly puts these in the

[6] In his discussion of the Ludlow occasion in his forthcoming biography of John Milton, which he kindly lent me in manuscript.

foreground. He provides the masque's characteristic pleasures of animating familiar reading and fusing creatures from it with shadowy presences of the local countryside. But beyond these pleasures, he provides Christian reference by pursuing in a masque the serious concern of Renaissance humanists to re-understand ancient myth in Christian terms. As an artist and entertainer, he begins with tangibles and opens out meaning through them. The environment of Ludlow Castle is extended in this way to reveal or express a Christian situation. By a daring coup, he uses for his purpose the custom of noble persons masquerading in ideal, exemplary roles: the fifteen-year-old daughter of the house will mime the virtue proper to her stage of life, Chastity; her brothers, the defense of chastity, the role Milton found so enthralling when as a boy he read romances. As the children "present" these parts, their own identities are to be extended, drawn out, educated. If their spiritual situation is understood, Milton's masque says, they are what they masquerade—even if they did not know it before Milton's project for them.

The finding of valid, Christian spiritual realities in classical myth was a great Renaissance enterprise; the high excitement of it is expressed by Thyrsis as he sets out to enlarge the Brothers' awareness of their situation:

> Ile tell ye, 'tis not vain, or fabulous
> (Though so esteem'd by shallow ignorance)
> What the sage poets taught by th' heav'nly Muse,
> Storied of old in high immortal vers
> Of dire Chirmeras and inchanted iles,

> And rifted rocks whose entrance leads to hell,
> For such there be, but unbelief is blind.
>   Within the navil of this hideous wood
> Immur'd in cypress shades a sorcere dwels.

To understand Milton's masque, we must be aware of the kind of moral and spiritual meaning which Christian humanism had been finding in classical myth for more than a century. Spenser's mythopoeia was in the foreground for Milton and his audience; but Spenser was part of a wide and complex tradition. Miss Tuve has beautifully exhibited the meanings which variations on the Circe myth were carrying; [7] she and Professor Woodhouse make clear how positive a virtue Milton was celebrating in presenting Chastity as an obligation of the natural order which could find sublime fulfillment in the order of Grace.[8]

But my concern here is to consider how, by the masque form, Milton brings such meanings into view. Dr. Johnson exhibited just the inappropriate assumption when he objected strongly against "the prologue spoken in the wild wood by the attendant Spirit" because it is addressed to the audience: "a mode of communication so contrary to the nature of dramatic representation, that no precedent could support it." [9] This astonishing lapse, which forgets so many instances in Shakespeare, results not only from Johnson's ignoring the masque form but also from the

[7] Rosemond Tuve, *Images and Themes in Five Poems by Milton* (Cambridge, 1957), pp. 112–61.

[8] A. S. P. Woodhouse, "The Argument of Milton's *Comus*," *University of Toronto Quarterly*, XI (1941–42), 46–71, and *"Comus* Once More," *University of Toronto Quarterly*, XIX (1949–50), 218–23.

[9] *Lives*, p. 98.

assumptions that go with a stage seen beyond a proscenium arch.
The audience, he insists, cannot be in the wild wood! A similar
assumption which relates to the whole problem of interpretation
appears in a recent extremely suggestive article by Professor
Sears Jayne, in which he proposes that Milton's machinery be
understood in terms of Ficino's Neoplatonism. Mr. Jayne sets
out by saying, "The *Mask* begins with a speech of the Attendant
Spirit in which he explains the setting, the world in which the
action of the masque is to take place." [10] He then argues that
Jove refers not to God but to the Neoplatonic World Soul, and
develops Ficino's systematic conception of the individual soul's
descent and return, a structure of thought which proves to have
fascinating parallels or potential parallels in Milton's masque.
What concerns me is not judgment among such possible meanings but the status they have in the work, the way the masque
reaches toward them. The Prologue does not once for all "explain
the setting, the world"; it only begins a process of opening up
which continues, dynamic and fluctuating, until the last lines of
the Epilogue. In the Prologue's first five lines we are made
aware that where we are is "this dim spot,/ Which men call
earth," that far above it are "regions milde of calm and serene
ayr," and beyond these, "the starry threshold of Joves court."
What are we to understand by Jove? At one moment less, at
another more, as the reach of the poetry moves through one
suggestion to another. We will be unaware of important meanings if we are not conscious of the systematic grids of Renais-

[10] Sears Jayne, "The Subject of Milton's Ludlow Masque," *PMLA*, LXXIV
(1959), 535.

sance thinkers. But the masque keeps moving in and out of them.
A slight hint that Milton was consciously concerned to keep clear
of too explicit Christian reference appears in one of his minor
revisions. In the Cambridge draft, the Lady, speaking of Chastity,
said

> I see ye visibly; and while I see ye,
> This dusky hollow is a Paradise,
> And heaven gates o'er my head.

This seems to have been rejected as too explicit, short-circuiting
a tension. In the way it advances through other symbols *toward*
the Christian, the masque is, surprisingly, not unlike *The Waste
Land*. The circumstances are vastly different; but both poets are
concerned to move through "secular" materials to mystery and
spiritual discovery.

Speeches seem too long when nothing seems to be happening.
Since in many of the speeches what is happening is the *creation*
of the situation, if we attend to that, instead of looking for the
forwarding of event, there is high excitement and delight. As an
example, consider the lines in which Comus tells the Lady that
he has seen her brothers, lines where the act of imaginative
creation is emphasized by the whole thing's being a downright
lie:

> Two such I saw, what time the labour'd oxe
> In his loose traces from the furrow came,
> And the swink't hedger at his supper sate;
> I saw them under a green mantling vine
> That crawls along the side of yon small hill,

> Plucking ripe clusters from the tender shoots,
> Their port was more than human, as they stood;
> I took it for a faëry vision
> Of some gay creatures of the element
> That in the colours of the rainbow live
> And play i'th plighted clouds. I was awe-strook,
> And as I past, I worshipt; if those you seek
> It were a journey like the path to Heav'n,
> To help you find them.

Comus' fabrication opens an exquisite vista, exactly in the manner of the masque. It is his supreme moment as a tempter, because a sight of her brothers is just what the Lady, prisoned from them in darkness, most desires. The "faëry vision" of "gay creatures" who can "play i'th plighted clouds' embodies the delight of perfect imaginative freedom, as in Shakespeare's Ariel. It is as though Comus gave the Lady a subliminal dose of his potion—and then he hypocritically steps into a posture of religious awe! Her response is to accept him as a guide.

III. Discovering the Resources of Chastity

To present a trial of chastity, the masque's way of moving by successive extensions of situation and awareness serves Milton perfectly. For preserving chastity involves keeping a relation with what is not present: the chaste person is internally related to what is to be loved, even in its absence. The experience of being cut off is wonderfully rendered by the poetry which creates the initial setting in the dark wood. The Lady's lines convey the disorientation that darkness can bring about, the thronging fantasies, and the soul's reaching out for objects of sight or sound through which to recover a relation to community. Her brothers, when they enter, express the same experience. "In double night of darkness and of shades," the Elder Brother longs for the sight of "som gentle taper":

> Though a rush candle from the wicker hole
> Of som clay habitation, visit us
> With thy long levell'd rule of streaming light.

In this situation, the young people's first resources are internal. The Lady reflects that she has with her still "a strong siding champion Conscience," and welcomes to her inward eye Faith, Hope, and "thou unblemish't form of Chastity"—"I see ye visibly, and now beleave."

The Elder Brother argues the power of Virtue with the Younger Brother in the "declamations" which irritated Dr. Johnson (and many a reader since):

> Vertue could see to do what vertue would
> By her own radiant light . . .

It is difficult not to hear Juliet's "Lovers can see to do their amorous rites/ By their own beauties"—and difficult to sympathize with the Elder Brother once we hear the echo. Certainly the least satisfactory part of the masque is this presentation, through the Elder Brother, of the resources which "divine philosophy" can provide for the defense of chastity. His speeches do tend to become dogmatic argument: in insisting on the autonomy of the individual will and spirit, he verges on a kind of hubris, so that we sympathize with the Younger Brother's practical concern about external dangers. To try to save the lines by making the presentation of the Elder Brother heavily ironic, as Mr. Hardy does, surely does not square with the fact that he expresses convictions Milton himself held. We are intended, I think, to feel a youthful absolutism, not unlike Milton's own as a boy reading romances. It seems to me that the response called for is not ironic rejection but tutelary approval blended with the sad amusement of experience watching innocence—the response of Thyrsis to the Elder Brother's fighting words about Comus:

> Alas good ventrous youth,
> I love thy courage yet, and bold emprise,
> But here thy sword can do thee little stead.

The Elder Brother's tone is less priggish if we keep his lines in context, feeling them as a reaching out for resources against the tensions of uncertain isolation. Frequently, dogmatism turns into something like invocation, the realization of imaginative realities:

> Do ye beleeve me yet, or shall I call
> Antiquity from the old schools of Greece
> To testifie the arms of Chastity?
> Hence had the huntress Dian her dred bow
> Fair silver-shafted queen for ever chaste.

Milton's marvelous power to slow down a line and dwell on its object brings Diana home as a presence, "Fair silver-shafted queen for ever chaste."

The outreaching gesture around which the first scene pivots is the invocation of Echo; Milton uses dramatically a standard feature of entertainments. The Lady's song "moves the vocal air/ To testifie his hidd'n residence"—it brings that physical resource into play. Nothing in the masque is more beautiful than the epiphany of the Lady's quality conveyed by the song and the descriptions of it. Comus acknowledges that

> such a sacred and home-felt delight,
> Such sober certainty of waking bliss,
> I never heard till now.

The nymph Echo does not answer the Lady; instead it is Comus who comes forward. But Thyrsis, high on "the hilly crofts/ That brow this bottom glade," also hears the song. And the Lady has the strength of assuming that her need *has* an Echo. One of the stunning things about the moment when she sings her song is that at such a moment she should sing such a song; she shows she is a Lady by presuming that she is in a world inhabited by "courteous" Presences:

> my severed company
> Compell'd me to awake the courteous Echo
> To give me answer from her mossie couch.

The act of singing is an exercise of the Lady's integrity; she is internally related, beyond the darkness, to what she looks to and realizes in the song. In the song is exquisite maidenliness— "sweetest nymph, that liv'st unseen/ Within thy airy shell"— along with a rich capacity for sensuous enjoyment and sympathy with passion: the Lady envisages Echo

> in the violet embroider'd vale
> Where the love-lorn nightingale
> Nightly to thee her sad song mourneth well.
> Canst thou not tell me of a gentle pair
> That likest thy Narcissus are?
> O if you have
> Hid them in some flowry cave,
> Tell me but where.

The contribution to Milton's sensibility of Renaissance aristocratic poetic traditions appropriate to the masque appears in the
contrast between the Lady's song and the more ungracious moments of the Elder Brother's exposition. The Lady's song does
not condemn amorous feeling in lines of moral firmness, addressed perhaps to "thou unblemish't form of Chastity"; instead,
its stanza so interwoven and complete holds a vision of delicate
eros. The Lady's shy capacity for love, attached at this moment
to her brothers, is expressed in Echo's living unseen within her
airy shell and yet perhaps hiding the brothers "in some flowry
cave." The result is dramatic rather than didactic composition;
for the Lady's vulnerability as well as her innocence is given
to the air by the song. Its strains

> float upon the wings
> Of silence, through the empty-vaulted night,
> At every fall smoothing the raven doune
> Of darknes till it smil'd.

Milton presents chastity not as a negative virtue but as an intact
disposition to love.

The preservation of chastity accordingly depends, his masque shows, not only on inner resources, crucial as these are, but on a world beyond the isolated individual and appropriate to the Lady's reserved ardor: there must be an actual echo. Comus provides a false echo, at first beautifully camouflaged, as we have seen, to fit the Lady's sensibility, later manifestly false in the enticements of his palace. Her security is partly in the strength of her will and the freedom of her mind. But more deeply it rests on the fact of there being other, worthy objects of love as alternatives to Comus' release. The ultimate object of love, the masque repeatedly hints, is heavenly—as in the song's final lines about Echo "translated to the skies," to "give resounding grace to all heav'ns harmonies." But on this side of heaven there is Thyrsis, at once a "glistring guardian" sent by "the Supreme good" and, in human terms, "my father's shepherd."

Here we should notice again what Milton does *not* do with the Christian supernatural. The role of the Attendant Spirit suggests at first affinities with those comedies where the action is overseen by a benevolent, omniscient figure who stage-manages it all: the Duke in *Measure for Measure,* Prospero in *The Tempest,* Reilly in *The Cocktail Party.* In such plays, the presiding figure tends to suggest Providence, and a special kind of humor arises from the contrast of his knowledge, which we share, with the ignorance in which the rest of the persons flounder about in the human condition. The perspective provided initially by Milton's Spirit serves in a somewhat similar fashion to give a background reassurance, furnishing perimeters within which the trial will take place. But it is striking that, once the action is started, the Spirit does *not* preside: he neither foretells what will happen nor speaks from behind his disguise to assure us that all will be well, as does such a figure as the Duke in *Measure for Measure*. The nearest he comes to this is in the narration telling of haemony to which Johnson objected "because it is false"! But here too there is no direct relation made to heaven or Jove's court: haemony is made the highest fruit of pastoral learning, the knowledge of simples. In the immediate context, this would include understanding of "dire chimeras," how they are and how they are not real. More simply, the herb serves as the embodiment of the resource which the presence of Thyrsis has given to the Brothers, and so completes the episode. Should we take it as Reason, or as Grace? There are associations with both, it looks *toward* both. That for the Brothers it does not entirely work fits with their incompleteness, and also with the further resource which the masque's progress will discover in Sabrina.

That the Attendant Spirit can become Thyrsis reflects the contribution of pastoral and the masque to Milton's art, an art here as elsewhere ultimately religious. The secular traditions provide mediating presences and objects between the human and the divine. One ground of this fortunate mingling of world and spirit was the aristocratic assumption of hierarchy, to which the masque was committed by its very nature as a genre devoted to compliment. A favorite pastime of the masque was "teaching difference," with moral superiority regularly linked—often factitiously enough—to social superiority. Frequently in court masques the antimasque was abruptly stopped by the arrival of some noble presence radiating awe, who would dismiss the antics from the hall with moral and aristocratic contempt. In *Pleasure Reconciled to Virtue,* Atlas dismisses in this fashion Ben Jonson's Comus, a simple god of gluttony, Shrove Tuesday style, with bottle-shaped followers.[11] Milton uses such a break, with rich complication, when his Comus, at the approach of the Lady, abruptly ends the dance of his followers (described as "a wild, rude and wanton antic" in the Cambridge manuscript).

The essence of this encounter of masquer with antimasque, translated by Milton's poetic and dramatic elaboration into a spiritual confrontation, is distilled in the recapitulation of the event which Thyrsis communicates to the Brothers in the second episode of the first scene. This second episode is beautifully designed: it repeats the movement the Lady has been through from isolation in darkness to an encounter opening out the situation toward a world of pastoral generosity; but the succor offered the Brothers is real, not Comus' "glozing courtesy." We re-experience the threat of intemperance from the perspective of the high lawns, in language which cues an active response. "Night by night/ He and his monstrous rout are heard to howl."

> And O poor hapless nightingale, thought I
> How sweet thou singst, how near the deadly snare!

What Milton made of the masque's movement, of the choreographic commonplace of a noble presence suddenly arresting the motion of the antimasque, is concentrated for me in a single

---

[11] *Ben Jonson,* ed. C. H. Herford, Percy and Evelyn Simpson (Oxford, 1941), VII, 482.

remarkable line of Thyrsis' narrative, "Till an unusual stop of
sudden silence." He tells how, his labors done, he sat down

> To meditate my rural minstrelsie,
> Till fancy had her fill, but ere a close
> The wonted roar was up amidst the woods,
> And fill'd the air with barbarous dissonance,
> At which I ceas't, and listen'd them a while,
> Till an unusual stop of sudden silence
>
> .   .   .
>
> At last a soft and solemn breathing sound
> Rose like a steam of rich distill'd perfumes,
> And stole upon the air, that even Silence
> Was took e're she was ware . . .

Of course the power or magic of such a line is implemented by
cadence, consonants, vowels: "*T*ill" with "*st*op" and "*sudd*en";
the undulations, between the stops, of "an unusual" and, after
them, of "silence." Without the form and pressure of the poetry,
the choreography would not carry; but the poetry is expressing
or implying choreography, a moment in a dance. One can imagine (though of course one does not need to) that a hand goes
up at "stop," a single dancer erect in warning above massed,
subsiding figures.

IV. The Masque as a Defense and Resource

We are now in a position to consider how Milton's use of the
masque form permitted him to order and satisfy feeling in an
entertainment presenting Chastity. In electing to make a Masque

of Chastity and put Revel in the role of villain, Milton undertook a particularly difficult task. Nobody but Milton would have
tried it! His sense of life prevented his using wholeheartedly one
of the great resources of entertainment literature, the release
sanctioned by seasonal or periodic holiday. On a tide of such
mirth, Shakespeare could move out into magic woods with an
implicit confidence in a return, after the holiday moment, with
humanity intact. It comes as a shock to hear the Lady speak of
country pleasures as "ill manag'd merriment." But what she has
actually heard is Comus' rout, who "night by night . . . are heard
to howl." Milton has deliberately presented a figure of Revel
who under the guise of refreshment tempts to dissolution from
which there is no coming back. The whole historical development of English life, regret it though we may, was giving ground
for Milton's new vantage toward the pleasures of Merry England.
The old agrarian housekeeping society, based on the land and its
seasons, was giving way to a dominant culture based on urban
conditions, where a leisure class would try to find, and others to
furnish, holiday pleasures everyday:

> when night
> Darkens the streets, then wander forth the sons
> Of Belial, flown with insolence and wine.

The first response which the attitudes of our own time suggest
is that Milton's project of celebrating Chastity is impossible. For
we not only have no cult of chastity, we have a cult of deflora-
tion. Crazy Jane, "Learned in bodily lowliness," tells the Bishop
that "nothing can be sole or whole/ That has not first been

rent." Much contemporary fiction is devoted to a mystique that spiritual exploration requires accepting one kind or another of rape by the world—or it laments the failure of this mystique. When we look at Milton in our psychological perspectives, we cannot help feeling that he was vulnerable, and that in his ideal-ization of chastity we have, clearly, a mechanism of defense. And yet, along with this sense of the artist and his subject, most of us find his masque wonderfully beautiful and satisfying.

One necessary way to understanding the poem's success is to consider what a positive conception chastity was in Milton's thought and in that of his time, as Mr. Woodhouse, Miss Tuve, and others have done. Through the ideal of chastity, Milton could reach to vital resources of his culture and religion. If Milton was vulnerable sexually, we should recognize that sexual vulnerability is just what his masque presents. If it is a defense, it is simultaneously a resource, a gathering of resources from a civilization which did not assume sexual invulnerability as an ideal. Milton fully recognized that unintegrated passion might destroy his particular complex sensibility, with its astonishing range of relation to psychic objects through which he achieved his sense of himself and of his relation to society and deity.

In *A Mask Presented at Ludlow Castle* he presents the pos-sibility of destructive release, and meets it by another sort of re-lease, the release of imagination carried by rhythm out and up to other objects of love. This alternative release is in its way physical, and so can work to counter that which Comus offers. For poetry and song *are* physical, the whole body engaged in the rhythms of articulation, envisagement centered in physical utter-ance. It is notable that the images which suggest a benign sexual release refer to song: "Silence/ Was took ere she was ware." In so far as the masque fails, it fails by a failure of rhythm. Where instead of poetry we get mere vehemence, mere assertion, and where our imagination is allowed to rest on the merely literal or merely intellectual contest, the defense of chastity lacks the final cogency of pleasure.

I feel a different sort of failure of rhythm in the speeches of Comus: much of his part seems too shallow rhythmically for the impact it should have, too stilted, as though Milton's auditory imagination could not risk getting more deeply involved. Milton certainly had a genuine artistic problem here; his whole design would not admit of Comus' capturing our imagination fully. His solution, so far as he does solve the difficulty, is to allow his god to revel, to begin each speech strongly, often beautifully, with appeals to the traditional sanctions, youth, feast, and nature's vital dance. Then he spoils it. Professor Joseph Summers, commenting on this difficulty I feel about Comus' part, writes that "I had always assumed that Milton *meant* us to have difficulty there—that the problem is not that Milton's auditory imagination could not risk getting more deeply involved but that he was trying to imitate precisely the failure of Comus' imagination—the mechanical movement and vulgar assumptions that his speech betrays." One can grant, as I do, that Milton's purpose required him to limit Comus in this way, yet a limitation still remains—a necessary limitation, but to be regretted nevertheless, as we regret Merry England. Autolycus can sing heart-whole of a liberty Milton's masque cannot include, a liberty which did not threaten Perdita's exquisite, passionate chastity.

Agreeing with Professor Summers, I find myself clear about

*dis*agreeing with the many critics who have read Comus' part with uninhibited delight, as though he were a more cultivated Autolycus. To take him without reserve, as though the release of the masque centered in his part, throws the whole out of balance. For if Comus persuades to a full release, there is nothing to resist him with but will, morality, principles.

The furthest reach of feeling, going out to the objects whose superior attraction defeats Comus, is in the Epilogue, where in the final version the imagination is carried beyond young Adonis and the Assyrian queen to celestial Cupid and "his dear Psyche, sweet entranced." The end of Chastity is love fulfilled, "Two blissful twins . . . Youth and Joy." Closer to the Lady's actual condition, and crucial in her rescue, is the figure of Sabrina, perhaps the most remarkable inspiration or revelation of the whole masque. Sabrina is, of course, exactly the sort of local genius looked for in noble entertainments; but Milton's astonishing mythopoeic power created almost all her particular qualities, qualities that are exactly, deeply right. The Lady is in a state of shock, following the attempted seduction. She cannot move, cannot go out to anything. What sort of figure can release her? Some presence identified with her father's power, the boundary of Wales. Some presence moist and cool—if the danger of seduction is melting heat, the danger of chastity is fevered desiccation. She cannot come out to her brothers, they cannot seize Comus' wand, because they are not men, and anyway they are brothers. A knight might take over from Comus, or, alternatively, a Vocation to the high mystery of virginity wedded to Christ. But a knight, or a Vocation, would take the Lady beyond the stage of life where she *is*. So the Sabrina who is invoked is a virgin who, threatened once, as the Lady has been, "still retains/ Her maiden gentleness." In the story of Sabrina's coming back to life, and the poetry and song which create her, we encounter, along with suggestions of the healing and renewing powers of water, the innocent cherishing of femininity by femininity, waiting and yet not waiting for another destiny, which is the proper resource of the Lady's stage of life:

> Sabrina fair
> > Listen where thou art sitting
> Under the glassie, cool, transparent wave,
> > In twisted braids of lillies knitting
> The loose train of thy amber-dropping hair.

Such is the power of the masque, in Milton's hands, to reach out and find, transformed, what, if embraced, is already there.

Isabel G. MacCaffrey

LYCIDAS: THE POET IN

A LANDSCAPE

Lycidas is both a great and complex poem, and a short one. It is therefore particularly attractive to the critic, its brevity making possible a unified single view and its compact intricacy inviting us to marvel at the sureness of technique that produced so expressive an order. Milton, the greatest architect in English poetry, never exercised his power to better effect. It is hardly strange, then, that we should view *Lycidas* as we regard some small but perfect building, say the Tempietto of Bramante in Rome. Its reticulated allusions and cross-referenced images, its "rhetoric of rhyme"[1] uniting the verse-paragraphs, perhaps above all its total familiarity, persuade us as critics to see in *Lycidas* a wholly visible, completed pattern.

Let us recall, however, a curious fact: *Lycidas,* almost alone among Milton's important poems, does not suggest at the be-

[1] F. T. Prince, *The Italian Element in Milton's Verse* (Oxford, 1954), p. 85. Prince discusses both atemporal effects of Milton's rhyme patterns—"rhyme which looks both back and forward"—and the creation of forward momentum through rhyme, "a sense of expectation" (pp. 86–87).

ginning how it will end. *Paradise Lost* unfolds its vast design in
the Argument and again in the opening sentences, laying before
us a fable whose concentric circles will widen steadily until all
its implications have been explored. The *Nativity,* another vision,
on a smaller scale, of a great nodal point of history, is also
concentric in its structure, beautifully suspending time in a series
of simultaneous visions. As we view it with a steadfast gaze, the
sun's wonted speed flickers and dies before the power of time's
maker and destroyer. *Comus,* like *Lycidas,* tells of a journey in
time; but, unlike *Lycidas,* it is provided from the start with a
cosmic setting in the opening speech of the Attendant Spirit. It
is thus defined as allegorical and exemplary, the Spirit relating
the poem to the audience's world and assuring us by his benefi-
cent presence that the outcome will be happy. In *Paradise Lost*
and the *Nativity,* again, Milton assumes the posture of a bard
whose formal utterance presents the poem to an audience and
who prophesies, in some degree, its conclusion.[2] All three poems
are mediated by a speaker who is not, or is not only, an actor
in the narrative. Even in *L'Allegro* and *Il Penseroso,* the poet
approaches at a leisurely pace, reciting genealogies before permitting us to hear with him the lark and the nightingale.

The opening of *Lycidas* is by contrast brutally direct. Declining
to observe the decorum of a public event, the poet in his Argument noncommittally recites the private occasion. His claim to
the role of prophet is modestly confined to immediate history;
he will foretell "the ruine of our corrupted Clergy." Of the
poem's conclusion we are given no hint, either in a formal presen-

---

[2] See Anne D. Ferry, *Milton's Epic Voice: The Narrator in "Paradise Lost"*
(Cambridge, Mass., 1963).

tation or in the painful emotions of the introduction. Nor does Milton explicitly take his bearings in the tradition of pastoral elegy, though he could easily have done so. One of his major models was Vergil's tenth eclogue, which is introduced by an appeal to the Sicilian Muse, a passage symmetrical with the conclusion imitated in the coda of *Lycidas*. But Milton does not allow us at once to place his poem in a literary context of mourning and consolation, nor does he permit us at the beginning a glimpse of that supernatural realm from which consolation will descend. Though the focus is on bucolic detail, it is the world of pastoral in general that he wishes us to assume, not any example of its literary embodiment that might cause us too readily to draw conclusions about what will happen next. The title and the word "Monody" in the Argument certainly offer clues to the poem's mode, and in line 10 the Vergilian echo admits a literary analogue more openly. But the design deliberately prohibits a large view, contrasting in this respect with the *Epitaphium Damonis*. There, Milton first invokes the *Himerides nymphae,* framing the picture of the poet under "the accustomed elm" with a formal introduction. The poem has a much less powerful forward momentum than *Lycidas;* the use of a refrain is one token that a movement of ebb and flow rather than sequence was intended. The voice speaks to us always from a little distance.

But in *Lycidas* we hear the unmediated exclamation of a speaker who is not yet identified as an uncouth swain. The mode is dramatic, hasting "into the midst of things," setting before us a moment of time in words that allude to prior events known to the speaker but not to us. "Yet once more" hints at other occasions on which laurel was plucked, but what occasions, whether personal or traditional, we are not told and we do not need to know. The opening words announce a proximate intention, insisting that we attend to a specific person about to perform a specific action. The details, while traditionally based, are minutely concrete and tactually realized in the modifiers "harsh" and "crude." We view the action from close up, as it moves urgently forward in time. This perspective is a circumscribed one in comparison with the ample horizons natural to Milton's imagination. We are related to this poem's action as eavesdroppers, ignorant, like the speaker, of where we shall finally emerge. *Lycidas* is, in short, a poem bound to the wheel of time, which is made to revolve before our eyes; we observe events as they occur, unfolding in the fictive span of the Doric lay from "Yet once more" to the swain's last words, in the future tense: "Shalt be good/ To all that wander in that perilous flood."

The landscape, the spatial coordinate, is present to register time's movement, which for the speaker, as for all of us, becomes visible when changes occur in the place where we are. The importance of a firmly established spatial foreground can be demonstrated by glancing at Milton's first English elegy, *On the Death of a Fair Infant Dying of a Cough,* a poem which the author, an exacting judge, excluded from the 1645 volume. This poem foreshadows *Lycidas* in the immediacy of its opening and in its reference to vegetation untimely cropt:

> O fairest flower no sooner blown but blasted,
> Soft silken Primrose fading timelesslie.

This is, however, precisely a poem *without* a landscape. Despite references to the seasons, there is no country where their sequences can be observed. Nor is there any spot where the speaker can establish himself as chief actor. He speaks from no place, and so the range of effective eloquence is severely limited for him; though there is plenty of movement, it lacks focus and therefore point. The poet has also neglected to provide himself with a metaphorical base, a fictive geography enabling the reader to assess the figurative weight of the conceits. Lacking the feigned literalness of "Yet once more . . . I come," the opening metaphor fails to evoke a world in which Hyacinth, Astraea, Winter, and Truth can live together. The address at the end to "the mother of so sweet a child" is disconcertingly abrupt; such a sudden emergence from fiction to fact need not occur in pastoral because the fiction is the fact incarnate. Initially literal, though preeminently metaphorical, the pastoral convention can assume much while saying little and yet permit elaboration of detail in a concretely realized foreground when that is appropriate.

So far, I have been trying to describe the kind of poem *Lycidas* is, and how Milton defines its genre obliquely in his mode of presentation. It is dramatic, unmediated, unfolding in time and in the space of a recognizable but, at the beginning, incompletely realized pastoral landscape.[3] A second question is, of course, implied: Why must it be so? To describe a form is

[3] "The poem is . . . clearly a dramatic lyric, with a setting, an occasion, a chief character, and several subordinate characters." M. H. Abrams, "Five Types of *Lycidas*," in *Milton's "Lycidas": The Tradition and the Poem*, ed. C. A. Patrides (New York, 1961), p. 222.

also to define a theme. In *Lycidas* is embodied one of the great
themes of poetry, one of crucial concern to Milton—the loss of
innocence. The prototype of this motif, as of so many others, is
definitively rendered in *Paradise Lost,* but it must undergo a
formal metamorphosis when treated on the private level in Milton's elegy. For fallen man, its essential meanings demand, and
here receive, a temporal development, an exposure of the process,
known to each one of us, by which innocence *becomes* experience.
In *Lycidas,* the process is generated by the sudden invasion of
the protagonist's consciousness by those great powers linked with
Time in another poem of the 1645 volume. With the advent of
"long Eternity," Milton wrote, we shall triumph at once "over
Death, and Chance, and thee O Time." [4] But eternity is not yet.
Death and Chance, united in the terrible figure of the blind
Fury, provide the occasion for the sequences of *Lycidas.* The
first loss of innocence brought Death into the world, and hence-
forward death is cause and symbol simultaneously of those repeated losses suffered by Adam's seed. [5]

Death is the occasion, lost innocence the theme; the poem

[4] *On Time,* lines 11, 22. The text of Milton's poems, including *Lycidas,* is
that of Helen Darbishire's one-volume edition in the Oxford Standard Authors:
The Poetical Works of John Milton (Oxford, 1958).

[5] The relation between the subject matter of *Paradise Lost* and of *Lycidas* is
illuminated by several of the other contributions to the memorial volume of
1638. For example, Henry King (brother of Edward) invokes Death as "execu-
tioner to destinie," the product of Sin, like other "tormentours" which also make
part of the subject of Milton's two poems:

> Brought in by sinne, which still maintains thee here,
> As famines, earthquakes, and diseases were,
> Poore mans tormentours, with this mischief more,
> More grievous farre, his losse whom we deplore.   (7–10)

Justa Edouardo King, ed. E. C. Mossner (New York, 1939), Part II, p. 1.

itself records the experience provoked by death and loss. The true landscape of *Lycidas* is the speaker's consciousness; as Northrop Frye has said, Milton "presents the poem as, in a sense, contained within the mind of the poet."[6] The action is epistemological before it is moral; the sin of the protagonist does not figure directly in it, as it does in *Paradise Lost*. Rather, like Blake's singers, the shepherd awakens from the dream of innocence to find himself living in a world of experience, a world of death, injustice, and sick roses, ruled by a blind Fury. Such an awakening occurs, of course, in every fallen human life, and must occur if we are to grow toward truth; but it is always painful. The speaker suffers, then, an unwelcome expansion of knowledge. How to cope with such knowledge is, indeed, a moral problem which the poem does not long evade.

Both the temporal and the spatial perspectives of *Lycidas* are designed to convey the implications of this awakening. The poem's threefold pattern has long been visible to critics: a "poetry" section, a "church" section, and a resolution. Many readers have observed too that *Lycidas* is only intermittently "pastoral"; the bucolic tone and rural setting are repeatedly left behind as new ranges of awareness open in the speaker's memory and imagination. This alternation of tones and landscapes reflects the two worlds of the poem: of innocence and of experience. The second invades the first, with effects of violation and distress, both emotional and aesthetic, that have caused commentators to speak

[6] "Literature as Context: Milton's *Lycidas*," *Fables of Identity* (New York, 1963), p. 122.

[7] The structure is clearly outlined by Arthur Barker, "The Pattern of Milton's *Nativity Ode*," *University of Toronto Quarterly*, X (1940–41), 171–72.

of "digressions." This now old-fashioned concept records a true response; in shifts of tone, setting, and temporal planes, Milton imitates a basic pattern of consciousness, the emerging sense of loss in all its catastrophic significance. The speeches of Phoebus and St. Peter, first heard in an unspecified past, are absorbed into the speaker's meditation, and each is followed by a return to a later point in the temporal "plot," as "now" moves forward to a new stage. There is a series of parallel returns in space to the pastoral landscape where fountains, rivers, and Muses mourn the dead shepherd, offering consolation which becomes more poignant but less satisfying as the poem develops.

In the first paragraphs of *Lycidas,* Milton makes two initial statements of the theme. The introductory lines put before us that interference with "nature" that has been immemorially a symbol of evil. In the proper order of things, berries ripen, leaves fall in their season, the year revolves in a "due" round. Milton's epithets—"harsh," "crude," "rude," "forc'd"—connote the disruption of macrocosmic decorum, insisted upon and indeed effected by a speaker accustomed to see his feelings reflected in the world around him. His forced fingers compel the season to recognize disaster. From this premature death, other disturbances must follow, though Milton does not admit the traditional extravagance of proclaiming that the young man's death *caused* nature's decay. "With him all things have died, even as he, and the flowers are all withered"; this is Bion's *Lament for Adonis,*[8] but the conceit is inappropriate for *Lycidas,* where the loss of

[8] Thomas P. Harrison, Jr., ed., *The Pastoral Elegy,* translations by H. J. Leon (Austin, Texas, 1939), p. 35.

innocence leads to a changed relationship between the speaker and "nature." Further on in paragraph 1, the wild fallen world beyond the pastoral island emerges, as we first glimpse the sea where Lycidas welters. This ocean is a "property" in the poem, a feature of the literal level; is is also connected, of course, with Milton's feelings about the uncontrollable events of human life.

The two worlds thus established in the opening images are further defined in paragraphs 3 and 4. A passage of reminiscence recreates, precariously, the world of "then"—before death, change, and the canker in the rose. It is the most complete rendering of landscape which the poem offers, and *at this point* in the "plot" exists only in memory, a never-never land which (the speaker believes) has disappeared forever. In its place is the fallen world of heavy change described in the next passage. But what precisely has changed? Surely the speaker's state of mind—not the landscape, but what his newly acquired experience causes him to see in it. So Eve sees, observing the sunrise for the first time with fallen eyes:

> see the Morn,
> All unconcernd with our unrest, begins
> Her rosie progress smiling.　　(*PL* xi.173–75)

The shepherd, even while he notes the sympathy of thyme and vine, strikes a similar (though not identical) chord.

> The Willows, and the Hazle Copses green,
> Shall now no more be seen,
> Fanning their joyous Leaves to thy soft layes.

Since Lycidas no longer sings, the willows cannot fan their leaves in harmony; but they are still *there*. The leaves may, even, still be joyous.[9] Two facts about "nature" becomes visible: a desolating unconcern with man, implicit in her ability to renew her life; and the fact that the only valid "sympathy" between macrocosm and microcosm must be based on their common corruption as fallen worlds.

The second of these insights is developed in a simile. Overt comparison is rare in this pervasively metaphorical poem. It suggests here a likeness between man and nature that is somewhat less complete than the identification of self and world recalled in the passage on the shepherds' unfallen pleasures. A new relationship, of similarity, not identity, is established. The literal landscape exhibits features *analogous* to the mind's landscape; its details are thus transformed into figures of speech.

> As killing as the Canker to the Rose,
> Or Taint-worm to the weanling Herds that graze,
> Or Frost to Flowers, that their gay wardrop wear,
> When first the White-thorn blows;
> Such, *Lycidas,* thy loss to Shepherds ear.

The world of "nature" can provide the materials for poetry, for the "melodious tear" that is the poem, because it shares with man his fallen condition. But because it is unaware of its own state, suffering but not perceiving its corruption, the song of nature cannot adequately record the meaning of human death.

The loss is principally a "loss to Shepherds ear," an invasion

---

[9] As J. H. Hanford noted long ago, "He does not dwell on the fiction that the natural objects express grief. . . . It is the description that we remember, not the conceit." "The Pastoral Elegy and Milton's *Lycidas,*" in Patrides, ed., *Tradition and Poem*, p. 35.

of consciousness, the subtly tuned ear of the mind. The death-haunted anguish of time's passage is a human pain, and so Adam speaks of it in *Paradise Lost:* "A long days dying to augment our paine" (x.964). For the singer of *Lycidas,* as for Adam and Eve, there is a poignant contrast between this long day and the sequence of days that wheels through the pastoral paradise. That was the world of innocence, the same as the one recalled for Hermione by Polixenes in *The Winter's Tale:*

> We were, fair queen,
> Two lads, that thought there was no more behind,
> But such a day to-morrow, as to-day,
> And to be boy eternal.[10]

Milton's long sentence holds in suspension the dream of eternal boyhood, a pattern, so he had thought, to be endlessly renewed.[11]

> Together both, ere the high Lawns appear'd
> Under the opening eye-lids of the morn,
> We drove afield, and both together heard
> What time the Gray-fly winds her sultry horn,
> Batt'ning our flocks with the fresh dews of night,
> Oft till the Star that rose, at Ev'ning, bright
> Toward Heav'ns descent had slop'd his westering wheel.

In the pastoral metaphor as Milton explores it in *Lycidas,* something of the life history of the convention is visible, and

[10] I.ii.62–65. Ed. A. C. Quiller-Couch and J. D. Wilson (2d ed., Cambridge, 1950).

[11] See Rosemond Tuve, *Images and Themes in Five Poems by Milton* (Cambridge, Mass., 1957), pp. 89–91. The present essay is heavily indebted to Miss Tuve's discussion of *Lycidas* in this volume—one of the most expert readings the poem has received.

not only in the many traditional details. Nostalgia has often been the sentiment that produces pastoral; almost since its earliest appearance, an innocent bygone virtue has implied a corrupt present sophistication, acquiring glamor by virtue of the contrast. The pastoral world becomes remote in space or time, or both, retreating to a legendary past or an imaginary country. So Arcadia is born. In *Lycidas,* this remoteness develops before our eyes, as the speaker's lost childhood is re-created in the past tense of memory. Pastoral perfection recedes into a past innocent and unreturning.

In *Lycidas,* too, we can observe the development of a so-called satirical element from the co-presence of harsh reality and benign past. Pastoral innocence provides an ethical measure for judgment and a technical point of departure for analyzing the ruined fallen world of experience. The beginning of such a process may perhaps be seen in Vergil's first eclogue, entitled in one modern translation "The Dispossessed." [12] One of the speakers is taking the rocky road to exile, stripped of his patrimony by a ravenous and unjust state. The other shepherd, Tityrus, has already endured voluntary exile in Rome, gained a protector, and returned to his farm.[13] Meliboeus' speech to him evokes a changeless peace:

---

[12] E. V. Rieu, *Virgil: The Pastoral Poems* (Penguin Books, London, 1949). The translated passage from the *Eclogues* below is taken from p. 23 of Rieu's edition. The Latin text is that of the Loeb Classical Library: *Virgil,* ed. H. R. Fairclough (2 vols., Cambridge, Mass., 1946).

[13] An apparent allusion to this eclogue in *Epitaphium Damonis* suggests that Milton took an interest in the pattern of exile and return. He speaks of his Italian journey, including the visit to Rome which is no longer "qualem dum viseret olim, Tityrus ipse suas et oves et rura reliquet" (ll. 116–17); even if a

Time and again, as it has always done, the hedge there . . .
will have its willow-blossom rifled by Hyblaean bees and coax
you with a gentle humming through the gates of sleep. . . .
You will hear the vine-dresser singing to the breezes, while
all the time your dear full-throated pigeons will be heard, and
the turtle-dove high in the elm will never bring her cooing
to an end.

The ceaseless country sounds, the suspension in a friendly element, are rendered by Vergil in words denoting time's recur-
rence: *nota, semper, nec tamen interea.* Yet the peace is shown
to be precarious by the presence of the exile and references to
wars in Africa, Scythia, Britain, even at home. Resolution, Vergil
implies, is won not simply by retreat but by a prior excursion into
and mastery of the "great world" outside. This reading of *Eclogue
I* is perhaps an overreading, but it illustrates how readily in
pastoral a suggestive contrast develops between a precious but
vulnerable rural landscape and a ferocious if sometimes heroic
world of history.

Lycidas reenacts, then, both the immemorial journey of the
maturing spirit and the development of one of humanity's most
resourceful metaphors for that journey. It is a poem "about"
poetry *and* "about" human life—about the two in conjunction,
man's vision of himself and the mirror of art in which he sees
the vision. It can be read as a reassessment of the pastoral mode
itself. Innocence is exchanged for bleak experience, in turn to be

reference to Chaucer is intended, behind it is surely Vergil's poem. In the
Epitaphium, the journey coincides with the death at home of Diodati; it is
thus linked with the "discovery" of the rude facts of life and death.

replaced by a wiser innocence. So "mere" pastoral—both the poetry and the view of the world it implies—is shown as too vulnerable and limited to account for the brutalities of life; but shown, finally, to contain the possibility of deeper, or higher, strains more faithful to "reality."

These intertwined threads of Milton's theme are visible in the details of the landscape picked out by the speaker. All four elements play a part in *Lycidas,* and all an ambivalent part, reflecting their divided allegiance in a fallen world where they may either serve as emblems of their Creator or become the playthings of satanic forces. Thus, Air is the "parching wind," the "gust of rugged wings," the figurative wind that bloats the sheep; [14] it is also the breezes in the willows, the "milde whispers" of valley winds. Earth puts forth the vegetation that can either flourish or wither. Fire is represented, on the one hand, by the counterfeit flare of fame's "sudden blaze," the "glistering foil" of worldly reputation; and, on the other, by the lofty light-bearing heavenly bodies: the evening star, and Phoebus who brings dawn and witnesses to the glory of the firmament. "Water imagery" in *Lycidas* has been sufficiently explicated; its doubleness should perhaps be more emphasized.[15] It is at once the monster-harboring, formless ocean that was to symbolize Chaos

---

[14] Ruskin's elaboration of ll. 125–27, developing the notion of *spiritus* or "wind" as breath, ought to be recalled: "There are two kinds of breath with which the flock may be filled; God's breath, and man's. The breath of God is health, and life, and peace to them, as the air of heaven is to the flocks on the hills; but man's breath—the word which *he* calls spiritual—is disease and contagion to them, as the fog of the fen." Lecture I, *Sesame and Lilies* (New York, 1866), p. 32.

[15] The contrast between sea water and fresh water was noticed by Emerson R. Marks, *Explicator,* Vol. IX (1951), Item 44.

in *Paradise Lost,* and the fountains, dews, and friendly rivers that mourn for Lycidas in the unsullied pastoral world. In the Alpheus/Arethusa references, the two strands meet but do not merge, and the resurgence of Alpheus from the dark descent beneath ocean's floor bears witness to the ultimate deliverance of creation from the dark forces that hold it enthralled. To look at these elemental patterns in the light of the poem's development is to see mirrored in them the movement of the speaker's mind. He reaches a point where the demonic aspect of creation dominates his consciousness. Experience has supplanted innocence, and the pastoral metaphor of a nature exactly congruent with man's life, responsive to his hopes and fears, has been revealed as inadequate.

In a passage from *Pericles* that was perhaps in Milton's mind when he wrote *Lycidas,* the king speaks to the "scarcely coffin'd" body of his wife and in his grief it seems to him that "th' unfriendly elements/ Forgot thee utterly." [16] We ought not perhaps to go so far as to speak of unfriendly elements in *Lycidas.* "Nature" is always "sympathetic" in the etymological sense, and Miss Tuve has wisely reminded us that we must beware of importing notions about man's alienation from nature into Renaissance poetry.[17] But just as the Muse can seem thankless, the elements can seem unfriendly to the speaker. They are related

---

[16] III.i.57–58. Ed. J. C. Maxwell (Cambridge, 1956). T. H. Banks observed that a manuscript phrase in *Lycidas,* l. 157—"humming tide" (altered to "whelming")—echoes *Pericles,* III.i.63: "And humming water must o'erwhelm thy corpse." Pericles' speech powerfully evokes the journey of Thaisa's dead body through the whales' "monstrous" realm. "A Source for *Lycidas,* 154–158," *Modern Language Notes,* LXII (1947), 39–40.

[17] *Images and Themes,* p. 95.

to us, we are made of them, yet they are powerless to help, just as "the Muse herself that *Orpheus* bore" was helpless to save him from death at the hands of arbitrary unintelligible forces. But these forces are outside the original economy of nature and cannot be ruled by it, as the speaker ultimately realizes. Of the paragraphs following the passage on "heavy change," one exonerates Nymphs and Muse of responsibility for Lycidas' fate; another speaks in defense of the destructive element itself:

> The Ayr was calm, and on the level brine,
> Sleek *Panope* with all her sisters play'd.

This "level brine" is an innocent extension of pastoral fields, the playground of nymphs. The accusation is diverted to the "fatall and perfidious Bark," belonging to the world of the blind Fury and her shears—a world of fallen, civilized, and unnatural contrivance and of mysterious subnatural hostilities alluded to in the eclipse, which in *Paradise Lost* gives evidence of nature's fall. These progressive exonerations are preparing for the final movement of *Lycidas,* into a "nature" hallowed and redeemed, a pastoral mode deepened and reconfirmed.

If nature is excused in *Lycidas,* however, man is not. The passages on Fame and the Church move away from the pastoral foreground into the vicissitudes of history and the consequences of our lost innocence. The embodiment of fallen society is the ominous blind Fury, a Fate rechristened but still as blind as her meaningless power.[18] In this section, as the poet's allusion to a

---

[18] Cf. Marjorie Nicolson, *John Milton: A Reader's Guide to His Poetry* (New York, 1963), p. 95, on the significance of the eyes of the Furies.

"higher mood" suggests, the style alters; and it can alter decorously because the matter alters. Milton begins in the pastoral present, referring to poetry as the "Shepherds trade." But the action moves immediately into a no-time of eternal verities and questions, and an infinite space where the great antagonists of the major poetry confront each other in the persons of the Fury and Phoebus. It is a metaphorical space inhabited by the august personages of sacred allegory, a world evoked at the opening of the *Nativity* Hymn and of *Comus,* where meek-eyed Peace and the Attendant Spirit make visible things ordinarily invisible to mortal sight. This is, in short, the plane of vision and prophecy, affording a glimpse of final verities ultimately to be affirmed in the poem and in history.

The debate of the speaker with Phoebus defines an aesthetic and moral issue. The lines on Fame, as Miss Tuve has said, use the language of chivalric romance—"guerdon," "foil," "spur," "noble mind."[19] The ambition to win fame by composing the poetry that celebrates earthly glory is shown by Phoebus to be a false direction; this is the same Phoebus, after all, who plucked Vergil's ear and reproved him for writing of "kings and battles" in *Eclogue VI.*[20] This ambition can also be seen as a betrayal of the values embodied in pastoral, which in Christian tradition encompasses both the lowest and the highest subjects. The shepherd singer of the Psalms is one exemplar, another "That Shep-

---

[19] *Images and Themes,* p. 74.

[20] It is interesting that, in the sixth eclogue, Vergil goes on to write, in Silenus' song, of subjects loftier and more permanently significant than battles: Creation, the Deluge, and the shifting shapes of mythological history. This poem, like *Eclogue IV,* provided Milton with a classical precedent for his development of "high pastoral."

herd, who first taught the chosen Seed" (*PL* 1.8) in the sacred poetry of Genesis. In *Paradise Regained,* Milton was to contrast Sion's songs with the "swelling Epithetes" of pagan poetry (IV.343). The contrast is confirmed in his rejection of traditional epic in favor of a heroic mode that would treat of virtues at once grander and humbler. The middle realm, the realm of history and its monotonous disasters, is the fallen world in the power of the Fury, recorded in an epic poetry corrupt though brilliant. Perhaps we should not press this point, which depends partly on our knowledge of the author's future, invisible to him in 1637. But the infirmity of ambition rebuked in *Lycidas,* whether poetic or heroic, is conceived in terms inconsistent with the pastoral metaphor.

A second vision of history is developed in the Church passage. As in the one just examined, this section is separated in time and space from the pastoral foreground. We move back or away from the "literal" landscape of rivers—Sicilian or English—and the classical allusions that enforce the pastoral mode, into a development of the convention's *metaphorical* dimensions, principally through the theological associations of "pastor." The figure of St. Peter emerges out of the pastoral world (like the "pastor" metaphor itself); it is continuous with the pageant of witnesses to nature's innocence: the Herald of the Sea, Hippotades, Camus, and then the Galilean Pilot. But the pageant, as it concludes, merges with an envisaged past and the spaces of imagination, and the style of Peter's speech, like that of the Fame meditation, is allusive and oblique, as the two-handed engine and its multitudinous glosses suggest. References to flocks and herdsmen link the speech metaphorically, indeed, with the paragraph early in the poem on the diseased landscape. This later passage sternly explains how that death-pervaded world of experience came into being. The source of contagion in flower and flock is not "innocent nature" but sin-ridden human beings, here monstrously reduced to "blind mouthes." The safe world of the "faithful Herdman" is invaded by their rapacity. Their grating songs contrast with Lycidas' soft lays, their hungry diseased sheep with the flock battened on the "fresh dews" of the water of life. The potent lines on inward contagion recall the "killing" canker that lays waste the shepherd's heart, or "ear." But while at that early stage no consolation beyond Nature's lament could be proposed, the dread voice of the Pilot here speaks in condemnation and prophecy, of the sword's readiness and a heavenly meed.

In the final paragraphs of the song, resolution and consolation are achieved and the validity of the pastoral mode is confirmed. But these certainties, like the other hard-won insights of the swain, emerge only at the end of the process which Milton called elsewhere "the perpetual stumble of conjecture and disturbance in this our dark voyage." [21] *Lycidas* imitates the painful, unsteady effort of imagination which alone, in our mortal state, can lead to vision. The sense of moving forward among the half-lights of the dark voyage is nowhere felt more powerfully than in the poem's last stages. We turn from a minute and loving attention to the details of pastoral landscape in close-up,

---

[21] *The Reason of Church Government*, in *The Student's Milton*, ed. F. A. Patterson (New York, 1933), p. 506.

to the gigantic horizons of distant seascapes, from the bottom of
the monstrous world to the heavenly hosts singing in their glory.
The sequence embodies those grand shifts of perspective which
Milton was to exploit in *Paradise Lost*.[22] It also renders metaphorically the fundamental pattern of Christian literature, a
movement through the tragic phase to an ultimately comic vision.

Accompanying this process is a sequence of imagery that
supports the movement of insight won, lost again, and rewon.
The kinetic and auditory images of Peter's speech are succeeded
by the "flower passage," a landscape rich in visual detail. Blind
Fury and blind mouths are replaced by a healthier world whose
moral value is symbolized by its appeal to the eye, though these
quaint enameled flower-eyes do not see as far as the "pure eyes"
of all-judging Jove, nor is the vision they symbolize finally valid.
In these low valleys, the gentle "nature" of the opening sections
emerges again: shades, gushing brooks, fresh fields. The "swart
Star" reminds us, however, of the flowers' frailty and their
melancholy fates—the primrose forsaken, the cowslips wan, even
Amaranth shedding his beauty in tribute to Lycidas. Since the
mortal sin, this is no plant that grows on mortal soil; it resembles
rather the plant of true fame that "lives and spreads aloft." In
Paradise Lost, Amaranth after the Fall is removed from Eden
to Heaven, where it "grows/ And flours aloft shading the Fount
of Life" (III.357). Its failure to thrive on earth marks the final
failure of unconsecrated pastoral in *Lycidas,* confirmed by the
speaker's acknowledgment that the whole vividly evoked scene
has been "false surmise," though its falseness to fact need not

[22] This use of rapidly shifting points of view is discussed and related to
Mannerist styles by Roy Daniells, *Milton, Mannerism and Baroque* (Toronto,
1963), p. 41.

negate the measure of imaginative consolation it provides.[23]
Pastoral as the dream of an actual earthly paradise is about to
be finally abandoned, but pastoral as a holy fiction foreshadowing a heavenly meed is about to be confirmed.

/ The song's conclusion is composed in two movements. The
first expresses the poem's deepest terror in a series of sensory
impressions that appeal to the dumb, blind responses of the
helpless body—not vision, but inhuman sounds and eyeless kinetic forces: "wash," "hurld," "stormy," "whelming." The speaker
does not withdraw his earlier assent to Neptune's plea of innocence; he does not accuse, but merely records the facts of Lycidas'
condition as they assault the anguished imagination. Then, almost without warning, the perspective shifts again, from the
blind depths to "the great vision of the guarded Mount," the
angel who fixes the sea's boundary and wields a two-handed
sword.

In *Paradise Lost,* Michael reveals to Adam the triumph of
Chaos in history, symbolized by the Deluge when the sea is
allowed to regain its power over the forces of order. Following
the vision he unfolds its meaning:

> So willingly doth God remit his Ire,
> Though late repenting him of Man deprav'd,
> Griev'd at his heart, when looking down he saw
> The whole Earth filld with violence, and all flesh
> Corrupting each thir way.   (xi. 885–89)

[23] In the Trinity MS, Milton first wrote "sad thoughts" in line 153. The
alteration to "fraile" (one of the crucial words in *Paradise Lost*) introduces the
notion of human weakness, in this case perhaps the habit of clinging to consoling fictions which we know to be untrue.

Violence and the corruption of all flesh: these have been revealed, with relentless insistence, to the swain in *Lycidas*. But
the rainbow speaks, in the epic, of reestablished order:

> Day and Night,
> Seed time and Harvest, Heat and hoary Frost
> Shall hold thir course, till fire purge all things new,
> Both Heav'n and Earth, wherein the just shall dwell.
>
> (XI.898–901)

In Books XI and XII, Milton develops on a grand scale the movement from disaster to redemption adumbrated in *Lycidas*. The
vision that completes the cycle of history in the epic completes
the cycle of meditation in the elegy.

The hinge of the transition from the infernal underworld to
the heaven of heavens is the Sun image, the second of the two
major similes in *Lycidas*. The ground of the analogy is the
circular solar movement, concentric with that of the dead shepherd, from ocean bed to morning sky. This parallel is profoundly
reassuring in its context—chiefly, I think, because it denies the
most poignant disparity between man and the nonhuman world:
for while seasons, stars, and vegetation move in cyclical patterns,
a man's life pursues an unreturning course downward to darkness. This distressing fact is lamented, of course, everywhere in
elegiac poetry: in Catullus' reminder that "one ever-during night"
awaits us, in Spenser's *November* eclogue, in Castiglione's *Alcon,*
where the sun comparison contrasts with that in *Lycidas:*

Behold, the declining sun now sinking in the heavens is setting, and as it dies, kindles the stars in the sky; still, when it

has bathed its chariot in the western waves, it will again re-visit the lands with orient light. But when once we have bathed in the black waters of cruel death and the door of that relentless realm has been shut, no way leads ever to the upper light.[24]

But Milton's conclusion reaffirms the congruence between nature's cycle and man's: Lycidas, *like* the daystar, is "sunk low but mounted high." The daystar itself functions in the poem not as a symbol but as an analogue; Milton wishes us to hold apart in imagination the various realms of being—natural, human, supernatural—precisely so that we can admire the marvelous correspondences between them. Therefore he makes the comparison overt, a simile, not an identifying metaphor. The diurnal cycle reminds us that something similar occurs for the youth sunk beneath ocean's floor, as earlier it occurred in the death and resurrection of God himself, who assumed the burdens and necessities of "nature" when he entered our darksome house of mortal clay. The simile, like the rose figure of an earlier section, at once affirms a distinction between ourselves and "nature," and reaffirms its ultimate relationship to us. We are able, owing to the song's last paragraph, to look back to earlier sections, especially the flower passage, and see them in a new light: the pathos and consolation did after all have a "real" basis, the flowers in their annual cycle are after all in harmony with the life of men. In this new perspective of analogy, "nature" is seen to possess a metaphorical relevance to human concerns; its availability for

---

[24] Harrison, ed., *Pastoral Elegy*, pp. 114–15.

Christian pastoral poetry is implied. But it *becomes* sentient and expressive only in the light of the poet's transforming vision.

The force that accomplishes these metamorphoses is the same that translates Lycidas: "the dear might of him that walk'd the waves." The redemptive power is figured in an image Milton had used earlier; in the *Nativity,* nature's most unruly force is hallowed by the Redeemer's coming, and "Birds of Calm sit brooding on the charmed wave" (Stanza V). The ruling of the waves was heralded in that mythic event when the creative Word ruled Chaos:

Silence, ye troubl'd waves, and thou Deep, peace.   (*PL* vii.216)

Christ's walking the waves possesses every kind of aptness in a poem about a drowned youth whose brief life embodied the forces of order implicit in his vocations of poet and priest. In eschatological terms, it defines the relationship between the Redeemer and redeemed Creation that permits the Christian poet to prefigure in his earthly landscapes those "other groves and other streams" of true paradise.

In the poem's temporal scheme, however, the redemption of nature is not final, and the speaker, who has descended and reascended in imagination, must be returned to his native element of life in time, like the Red Cross Knight after his vision of the New Jerusalem, or Calidore when the Graces vanished. The metamorphosis of Lycidas effects this return. He becomes, as Mr. Frye has said, a figure "corresponding to the Attendant Spirit in *Comus,* whose habitation is said to be a world above our own, identified . . . with Spenser's Gardens of Adonis." [25]

[25] *Fables of Identity,* p. 122.

As the Genius of the shore, he will mediate between the still fallen world of the perilous flood and the realm of redeemed nature glimpsed by the speaker in vision. He is the third, and most consoling, of the "heavenly messengers" who descend to the protagonist of *Lycidas*.[26] He will serve as a reminder that the wilderness of the world can be ordered and transcended.

The speaker in *Lycidas* has traveled from a preoccupation with the "melodious tear" of his song as the only possible "meed," to the vision of redemption where there are no tears, where the earthly shepherds weep no more and the song will cease, stilled by the unexpressive heavenly harmonies. The song ceases, but it has not been sung in vain. Its meaning is confirmed in the receding perspective of the coda which offers us, now more distantly but also more distinctly, a figure in a landscape, long familiar but now transfigured, *because* the song has been sung and the vision realized. The pastoral scene is re-created; and now it is informed by the presence of the poets who first made these details into poetry, and by the redeemed imagination that has come gradually to understand their meaning. The ancestor of the coda is Vergil's tenth eclogue, concluding traditionally with a return home and the arrival of the evening star. Line 190 of *Lycidas* echoes the conclusions of two other eclogues, where the sun stretches out the hills:

et sol crescentis decedens duplicat umbras.[27]

[26] Thomas M. Greene, *The Descent from Heaven* (New Haven, 1963), treats the "heavenly messenger" as a recurrent motif in epic. In *Lycidas*, the three "messengers"—Phoebus, Peter, and the dead shepherd as Genius—enter the poem just at those points where the "old" pastoral idiom is left behind and a new perspective into the heroic finalities of Providence is opened.

[27] *Eclogue II*, l. 67. The other echo, regularly noted by editors, is of *Eclogue I*, l. 83: "maioresque cadunt altis de montibus umbrae."

These deliberate allusions to literary tradition underline the function of the stanza as a "return": a return to the pastoral landscape and the poetry based on it, now made potent as a vehicle of human meaning because its patterns are seen to be reproduced in the divine plan of the universe. Like the young shepherds of the poem's third section, this uncouth but more experienced swain has piped through the wheel of a day, from still morn to westering sun. The last line is not to be read only as a personal reference to sea voyaging or a promise of the turn to epic poetry. "Fresh" and "new" surely reaffirm those self-renewing powers of "nature" that legitimately figure our own survival and revival. As for "tomorrow," it marks the return of a world where the future once again exists full of promise, not a long day's dying, but "such a day tomorrow as today," a process endlessly renewed by the covenant of God himself. In this world will flourish, not eternal boyhood, but a wise innocence that has absorbed and transcended experience. So Spenser's Colin Clout, after the manner of Tasso's shepherd, came home again from court. This new wisdom understands the pastoral world for what it is—a foreshadowing, not an echo. In this peaceful order, "Seed time and Harvest, Heat and hoary Frost/ Shall hold thir course," until the kingdom which the metaphor anticipated is established to succeed the cycles of history.

A decade or so before *Lycidas,* Milton in a Latin poem had celebrated the regular cycles of the universe and affirmed the eternal youth of great Nature, the perpetual flame of bright Phoebus in his strength: "floridus aeternum Phoebus juvenile coruscat." The poem concludes with an anticipation of Michael's revelation:

Sic denique in aevum
Ibit cunctarum series justissima rerum.[28]

"The righteous course of all things": it is precisely this sense of
control and ultimate rightness that Milton seeks to establish
in the final cadences of *Lycidas*. The voice that asserts it is impersonal. Many reasons for Milton's shift to the third person in
the coda can be reconstructed by the ingenious critic. Among
them is the fact that his subject at this point has transcended the
personal. Two others are pertinent to this discussion.

The first concerns the redefinition of pastoral convention. The
two similes, as I have suggested, are strategically placed in the
fourth and last paragraphs of the song; they record a development
in the speaker's treatment of his metaphor, from the naïve assumption that it represents actuality, to the recognition of it as
one of man's great symbols for ultimate reality, securely rooted
in the imagination's life. This insight is confirmed by the osten-
sive gesture of the poet in the coda. He can now name the poem's
"kind" explicitly: it is a *"Dorick* lay" sung by a swain. In thus
specifying its genre, Milton insists that pastoral be taken seriously. Like the swain, we must readjust our notions of what
"pastoral" can mean. It is to be recognized as a serious *fiction,*
a mode of the imagination, not a self-deluding fancy. The lowest
of forms has been demonstrated to be capable of articulating the
loftiest insights, embodying that vision of final things from which
Milton was to make *Paradise Lost*. This "high pastoral" is akin
to the metamorphosed epic form which Milton later devised for
an action more heroic than any known to Homer. In the prologue to Book ix, he was to announce his intention, defining

[28] *Naturam non pati senium,* ll. 41, 65–66.

the "Heroic name" of his poem as once he had directed attention to a new meaning of the Doric lay. The habit of transcending and transforming genres is most dazzlingly manifested, in the 1645 volume, in *Lycidas*.

Finally, the coda demonstrates the relevance, not only of the poem's form, but of its theme, to ourselves. As the impersonal voice addresses us, we become co-listeners, and as the foreground recedes into the middle distance we find ourselves paradoxically in a more intimate relation to it. This sensation is effected—I do not say intended—when the poem's frame unexpectedly widens to include the "real" speaker and ourselves, on the same footing because we have heard the same song. The poem's world becomes our world, the song's pattern a paradigm of our experience. In the final lines there is a fusion of worlds created by a confusion of temporal planes, phrased in syntax that unites past and present: "now had stretch'd," "now was dropt." Past and present are one, the song continuing though the singer has ceased. The last line refers ambiguously to the singer's thought, the poet's comment on his future, the author's prospects, and our own hopes.

> To morrow to fresh Woods, and Pastures new.

It is not unmistakably located "in" the mind or spoken by the voice of either the real or the fictive speaker, and can therefore sum up a pattern now possible for all those who, by listening, have participated in the song.

II

SAMSON AGONISTES

William G. Madsen

FROM SHADOWY TYPES

TO TRUTH

In recent years critical interest in *Samson Agonistes* has shifted from the question whether the play has a middle to the question of the play's theme and its relation to the other works of Milton's maturity. The terms Hebraism and Hellenism, which once figured so prominently in discussions of the theme, have all but disappeared, and it is now fashionable to speak of this classical tragedy with an Old Testament folk hero as Christian. Its spirit is "religious and Christian"; it is "a classical tragedy with a Christian theme and outlook"; it is a "remarkable blend of Greek form with Christian content"; Samson himself is "an heroic figure as conspicuously modern, Christian, and Miltonic as it is Hebraic"; *Samson Agonistes* is really *Christus Agonistes,* and the agony of Samson is a "surrogate for the unbloody sacrifice of the Mass." [1]

[1] Walter Clyde Curry, *"Samson Agonistes* Yet Again," *Sewanee Review,* XXXII (1924), 351; A. S. P. Woodhouse, "Tragic Effect in *Samson Agonistes," Uni-*

The fact that Milton was an avowed Christian poet obviously gives this view a good deal of antecedent probability; still, *Samson Agonistes* does not read like a Christian play: it is very difficult to transmute the muscular Samson into a Christian athlete, and even more difficult to make Christians of Manoa and the Chorus, from whose mouths proceed all the reflections on the meaning of Samson's tragedy. Critics who are not themselves Christians, or who wrote before Christian orthodoxy once again became intellectually respectable, have felt themselves under no compulsion to Christianize the play. Tillyard saw in it a "settled ferocity, not very lovely," although he was willing to admit Christian strains alongside the Stoic ones. Hanford went so far as to say that *Samson Agonistes* proves that Milton did not think that Christ's sacrifice was a necessary instrument of salvation; even Christ's example, it appears, might be dispensed with by those who enjoy a direct and special relation with the Divine. More recently Arnold Stein's analysis of the play contains not a single reference to Christ or Christianity. (Stein's, however, is a special case, for his interpretation, as I hope to show, is the most profoundly Christian of all.) [2]

How one relates *Samson Agonistes* to *Paradise Lost* and *Paradise Regained* depends to some extent on whether or not one

---

versity of Toronto Quarterly, XXVIII (1959), 222; Kenneth Muir, *John Milton* (London, 1955), p. 183; E. M. Clark, "Milton's Conception of Samson," *University of Texas Studies in English*, VIII (1928), 99; T. S. K. Scott-Craig, "Concerning Milton's Samson," *Renaissance News*, V (1952), 46–47.

[2] E. M. W. Tillyard, *Milton* (London, 1930), pp. 333–34; James Holly Hanford, *"Samson Agonistes* and Milton in Old Age," *Studies in Shakespeare, Milton and Donne* (New York, 1925), p. 177; Arnold Stein, *Heroic Knowledge* (Minneapolis, 1957).

regards the play as Christian, but there are problems enough in either case. Tillyard sees in it evidence that Milton had regained his faith in action after the quietism of *Paradise Regained;* Maynard Mack sees no conflict but rather a reconciliation of the competing ideals of action and contemplation. Woodhouse does not think a work so divergent from *Paradise Regained* in "doctrine, temper, and tone" could have been written at the same time and consequently dates *Samson* in 1660–61, the period of Milton's greatest disillusionment. Others, however, see it as a kind of companion piece to *Paradise Lost* and *Paradise Regained* in that it presents a "pattern-hero" who differs from Abdiel and Christ only in being more fully human and whose regeneration is thus a more compelling example for us fallen sons of Adam.[3]

It is ironic that a work whose simplicity and straightforwardness is often commented on should have given rise to such divergent and even antithetical judgments. There are those, no doubt, who would attribute this fact to the well-known tendency of Milton scholars toward special pleading—the problem of belief seems to arise in an especially acute form when Milton is being discussed—but I would attribute it rather to a failure to realize that *Samson Agonistes is* complex in a special way. I shall suggest that it is both non-Christian and Christian in much the same way as the Old Testament may be considered both non-Christian and Christian; and that it is, or at least may be re-

---

[3] Tillyard, *Milton,* p. 328; Maynard Mark, ed., *Milton* (Englewood Cliffs, 1950), p. 28; A. S. P. Woodhouse, "*Samson Agonistes* and Milton's Experience," *Transactions of the Royal Society of Canada,* 3d ser., XLIII, Sec. 2 (1949), 157–58; M. M. Mahood, *Poetry and Humanism* (New Haven, 1950), p. 211.

garded as, a companion piece to *Paradise Regained* and *could* have been written at the same time, even though it is remarkably different in "doctrine, temper, and tone."

The key to an understanding of *Samson Agonistes* is the method of biblical interpretation known as typology. In its narrowest sense the theory of typology states that certain persons, things, and events of the Old Testament are symbolic prefigurations, foreshadowings, or types of certain persons, things, and events of the New Testament. Thus Joshua is a type of Christ (the antitype); the synagogue a type of the Christian church; the sacrifice of Isaac a type of the Crucifixion. Sometimes the antitypes are not limited to the New Testament but extended to the whole Christian church and its members. The exodus of the Jews from Egypt to the Promised Land may be regarded (as it was by Dante) as a type of the journey of every Christian soul from the fleshpots of this world through the wilderness of self-denial and suffering to the Promised Land of Heaven. Some theologians have regarded certain persons and events of the New Testament as types whose antitypes are to be found in the future history of the Church. The method can even be extended beyond the confines of the Bible to encompass pagan history and literature. Dante regarded the Roman Empire as a foreshadowing of the Catholic Church, and Renaissance Neoplatonists were fond of seeing in Hercules a type of Christ and in pagan sacrifices a foreshadowing of the Mass.

Typological interpretation of the Old Testament was universally practiced by both Protestants and Catholics in Milton's day, and it fell into disuse only in the eighteenth and nineteenth centuries. It has recently enjoyed a revival among theologians, although there is nothing like general agreement about how it is to be applied or even about its general validity as a mode of interpretation. Some modern theologians reject it altogether; others would limit the Old Testament types to those explicitly mentioned in the New Testament; a minority feel free to exercise their own critical judgment or ingenuity. We need not concern ourselves here with the technical rules for discovering types laid down by theologians. The following observations, derived from a study of the types commonly accepted by Milton's contemporaries, will be sufficient for our merely literary purpose:

1. A type is a historical person or event, not a mythical person or a recurrent event like the rising and setting of the sun.

2. A type looks forward in time, not upward through the scale of being. The theory of typology is thus firmly grounded in the Judaeo-Christian world of existences and is fundamentally alien to the Greek world of essences.

3. Natural objects may be types, but they are usually such only in special historical circumstances. St. Paul tells us that the rock that Moses struck was Christ (the water that issued forth was regarded as a type of the blood and water that flowed from Christ's side when it was pierced by the spear); this does not mean that every rock is a type of Christ.

4. There must be differences as well as similarities between a type and its antitype. (A most important rule for *Samson,* as we shall see.)

5. Neither the actors of a typical event nor the authors of their history understand the typological significance of what they are doing or writing. The Jews wandering in the wilderness did not know that manna prefigured the Eucharist, nor did Joshua know

that in leading his people into the Promised Land he was a type
of Jesus leading his people into Heaven.

6. Hence, the meaning of a type cannot be known until it has
been fulfilled in its antitype.

Although Milton is often credited with a strictly rationalistic
theory of biblical interpretation, references to the doctrine of
typology may be found in writings from all periods of his life.
In *The Reason of Church Government* he says that "all those
sumptuous things under the law, were made to signify the inward beauty and splendor of the Christian church," and he
draws an elaborate analogy between the new temple described
in the prophecy of Ezekiel and the soul of man, which is God's
"rational temple." [4] In *Paradise Lost* Michael explains the significance of the Law to Adam in these words:

> So Law appears imperfet, and but giv'n
> With purpose to resign them in full time
> Up to a better Cov'nant, disciplin'd
> From shadowy Types to Truth, from Flesh to Spirit,
> From imposition of strict Laws, to free
> Acceptance of large Grace, from servile fear
> To filial, works of Law to works of Faith.   (xii.300–306)

What has this to do with Samson? Critics as different in their
assumptions and methods as Hanford, Krouse, and Woodhouse
agree that Milton did not present Samson as a type of Christ.
It is true, of course, that there are no explicit references to Sam-

---

[4] *The Reason of Church Government*, I.ii, in *John Milton: Complete Poems
and Major Prose*, ed. Merritt Y. Hughes (New York, 1957), pp. 645–46. All
quotations from Milton are taken from this edition.

son as a type of Christ. How could there be when the words of
the drama are confined to Old Testament actors? The meaning
of a type cannot be known until the antitype has been revealed,
and Samson and Manoa and the Chorus know nothing of Christ.
That there are, in fact, implicit foreshadowings of Christ in Milton's Samson I shall suggest in a moment; perhaps it is even
more important for an understanding of Milton's conception of
Samson, however, to recognize the differences between them, for
it is essential to the whole doctrine of typology that the type be
different from as well as similar to the antitype.

The major differences between Samson and the Christ of
Paradise Regained can be summed up as action vs. passion and
letter (or flesh) vs. spirit (or word).

Just after Harapha leaves, the Chorus exults in the return of
Samson's heroic vigor:

> Oh how comely it is and how reviving
> To the Spirits of just men long opprest!
> When God into the hands of thir deliverer
> Puts invincible might
> To quell the mighty of the Earth, th' oppressor,
> The brute and boist'rous force of violent men
> Hardy and industrious to support
> Tyrannic power, but raging to pursue
> The righteous and all such as honor Truth. (1268–76)

Mindful of Samson's plight, however, the Chorus goes on to
suggest that his vocation may be that of the patient sufferer:

> But patience is more oft the exercise
> Of Saints, the trial of thir fortitude,
> Making them each his own Deliverer,
> And Victor over all
> That tyranny or fortune can inflict.
> Either of these is in thy lot,
> *Samson,* with might endu'd
> Above the Sons of men; but sight bereav'd
> May chance to number thee with those
> Whom Patience finally must crown.   (1287–96)

The vaguely Christian connotations of the words "saints" and "patience" should not blind us to the essentially Stoic quality of the idea of victory over fortune, lot, and chance. Even if one should insist on regarding this passage as Christian, it is clear that Manoa and the Chorus finally regard Samson as an active, not a passive, hero:

> O dearly bought revenge, yet glorious!

Manoa echoes the Chorus' thought:

> *Samson* hath quit himself
> Like *Samson,* and heroicly hath finish'd
> A life Heroic, on his Enemies
> Fully reveng'd hath left them years of mourning.
>   (1709–12)

Samson's death was of a piece with his life, and his memory will inflame the breasts of the valiant youth of Israel "To matchless valor, and adventures high" (1740).

One such valiant youth was the young Jesus of *Paradise Re-gained*. Although he does not mention Samson in his soliloquy in the desert, the example of an earlier deliverer springs readily to mind when he says:

> yet this not all
> To which my Spirit aspir'd; victorious deeds
> Flam'd in my heart, heroic acts; one while
> To rescue *Israel* from the *Roman* yoke,
> Then to subdue and quell o'er all the earth
> Brute violence and proud Tyrannic pow'r,
> Till truth were freed, and equity restor'd.   (1.214-20)

These are precisely the terms the Chorus had used in the passage about the active hero quoted above, and Samson too had spoken of his own "great exploits" (32) and "mightiest deeds" (638) and of the promise that he "Should *Israel* from *Philistian* yoke de-liver" (39). The similarities, however, only heighten the great and significant difference: the aspiration to victorious deeds is an early stage of Christ's spiritual development; it is, in fact, one of the temptations of Satan, who is the great celebrator of heroic action in *Paradise Regained*. Satan tells the devils that Christ is adorned with "amplitude of mind to greatest Deeds"; his mind, more exalted than Solomon's, is "set wholly on the accomplishment/ Of greatest things." Later he tells Christ, "all thy heart is set on high designs,/ High actions," and the heroes he proposes for imitation are all men of action: Alexander, Scipio Africanus, Pompey, Julius Caesar, and Judas Maccabaeus, who retired to the desert with arms; we would hardly be surprised if Satan were to add the name of Samson to this list. Satan's understanding of Christ's role as the deliverer of Israel is like Samson's understanding of his own role, and when Satan appeals to Christ's sense of zeal and duty by recounting the abominations inflicted on Israel by the Romans, he too echoes the Chorus in *Samson* when it speaks of "Tyrannic power . . . raging to pursue/ The righteous and all such as honor Truth" (1275–76).

Samson's inability to rise to Christ's contempt for "ostentation vain of fleshly arm" (III.387) is underlined by Milton in the Harapha episode. Whether or not we regard Harapha's visit as a temptation, it is clear that Samson's response is seriously flawed. Wholly admirable is his trust in the living God, his willingness to acknowledge that God has inflicted these indignities on him justly; less admirable, at best, is his eagerness to engage Harapha in single combat, his pathetic belief that by clubbing Harapha to death he will demonstrate the glory of God. The language of chivalric combat used by both Samson and Harapha places this encounter at a vast moral distance from the "great duel, not of arms" in which Christ engages the Father of all the giants of the earth. Samson, it is true, has purified his motives since the time when "swoll'n with pride" he walked about "like a petty God . . . admir'd of all and dreaded" (529–32). But while purity of heart is a necessary part of the "wisdom" that vanquishes "hellish wiles" (*PR* 1.175), it is not enough. After all, some at least of the motives that Satan proposed to Christ were beyond reproach.

A more fundamental contrast between Samson and Christ is comprehended in Michael's lines quoted earlier:

> So Law appears imperfet, and but giv'n
> With purpose to resign them in full time
> Up to a better Cov'nant, disciplin'd
> From shadowy Types to Truth, from Flesh to Spirit.

Throughout his life Milton opposed to the literalism and carnality of the Old Testament the spirituality of the New. It is the basis of his attack on the bishops, whom he calls Judaizers and whose altars and candles at noon he says were "superstitions fetched from paganism or Jewism." [5] The Jews of the Old Testament, according to Milton, were content to remain in the letter of the law and did not realize, for example, that the ceremonial vestments were merely typical foreshadowings of the inward purity of Christians.

In *Paradise Regained* it is primarily Satan who represents the fleshly, literalistic Old Testament point of view. Someone has wittily observed that the trouble with Satan is that he cannot recognize a metaphor. The most obvious example is his failure to understand the significance of the Dove. When he was at the baptism, he tells his followers, he saw Heaven unfold her crystal doors and on Christ's head "A perfect Dove descend, whate'er it meant." Christ, on the other hand, knows perfectly well what it meant:

> But as I rose out of the laving stream,
> Heaven open'd her eternal doors, from whence
> The Spirit descended on me like a Dove.   (1.280–82)

---

[5] *The Likeliest Means to Remove Hirelings,* in Hughes, ed., *John Milton,* p. 865.

In the temptations that follow, Christ's strategy with Satan is
to internalize and spiritualize Satan's terms by turning them
into metaphors. And Satan is so literalistic that he can't even
understand a metaphor when it is explained to him. To his suggestion that Christ turn stones into bread to relieve himself and
others in the wilderness with food, Christ replies, "Is it not
written . . . Man lives not by Bread only, but each Word/ Pro-
ceeding from the mouth of God . . . ?" And a little later he
contrasts God's word to the words that proceed from Satan's
oracles: "For lying is thy sustenance, thy food." But Satan returns next morning to appeal to Christ's physical hunger, telling
the devils,

> And now I know he hungers where no food
> Is to be found, in the wide Wilderness.

But Christ, we know, is "fed with better thoughts" and is "hung-
'ring more to do [his] Father's will" (11.258–59). When he tells
Satan he has no need of food, the arch-literalist is baffled. "How
hast thou hunger then?" he asks (11.321), and proceeds to dis-
play his ludicrous baroque banquet. Christ counters with an
oblique reference to the Eucharist:

> I can at will, doubt not, as soon as thou,
> Command a Table in this Wilderness,
> And call swift flights of Angels ministrant
> Array'd in Glory on my cup to attend,   (11.383–86)

and ends with a contemptuous question,

> And with my hunger what hast thou to do?   (11.389)

In the temptation of the kingdoms that follows, Satan clings to his literalistic Old Testament interpretation of the role of the Messiah. Christ tells him, before the temptation is well under way, that he who reigns within himself is more a king; that to guide nations in the way of truth is yet more kingly; and that "to give a Kingdom hath been thought/ Greater and nobler done, and to lay down/ Far more magnanimous than to assume." But Satan hears not; he merely shifts his ground from means to motives. He appeals to Christ's sense of glory and then to his zeal and duty "to free/ Thy Country from her Heathen servitude." Christ has a conception of spiritual liberty and servitude far beyond Satan's ken:

> Should I of these the liberty regard,
> Who freed, as to their ancient Patrimony,
> Unhumbl'd, unrepentant, unreform'd,
> Headlong would follow, and to thir Gods perhaps
> Of *Bethel* and of *Dan?*   (iii.427–31)

But Satan persists, suggesting that Christ might ascend the throne of Tiberius and "A victor people free from servile yoke" (iv.102). "What wise and valiant man would seek to free/ These thus degenerate, by themselves enslav'd," asks Christ, "Or could of inward slaves make outward free?" (iv.143–45). The baffled Satan makes one last effort of the imagination. Christ seems "otherwise inclin'd/ Than to a worldly Crown," and Satan suggests to him that, as his empire must extend, "So let extend thy mind o'er all the world," ruling the Gentiles by persuasion. But this is the furthest Satan's mind will stretch, and when Christ rejects the learning of Athens, Satan admits he does not understand whether Christ's kingdom will be "Real or Allegoric." The joke is on Satan, as Northrop Frye has shown us, for Christ's kingdom, allegoric to Satan, is the only kingdom that is real.[6]

One way of defining Christ's strategy in *Paradise Regained* would be to call it a purification of the word. "In the beginning was the Word, and the Word was made flesh." Milton would add to this formula, "The Word was made flesh so that flesh might become word." In *Paradise Lost* when Christ incarnates himself he does not lessen or degrade his nature, but rather raises human nature to the level of divinity; when Satan incarnates himself in the serpent, he merely imbrutes his own essence.

If we turn now to *Samson Agonistes,* we will find no such metaphorical activity; at the most stones are turned into bread, but physical hunger is not transmuted into spiritual hunger. The two major motives of blindness and delivery from bondage receive only a limited metaphorical extension that falls far short of Christ's achievement in *Paradise Regained.*

Samson, for example, has insight enough to recognize that his present servitude is not so ignominious as his servitude to Dalila, and he can see that the Israelites were brought to servitude by their vices and hence prefer "Bondage with ease" to "strenuous liberty" (271), but he still thinks it possible "of inward slaves [to] make outward free" (*PR* iv.145). The insights of the Chorus are on a lower level: they regard Samson's blindness as a "Prison within Prison" (153), and they suggest that the man who can patiently endure what chance inflicts is the deliverer of himself.

[6] Northrop Frye, "The Typology of *Paradise Regained,*" *Modern Philology,* LIII (1956), 231.

Manoa's apprehension is the most earthly and literalistic of all as he pathetically and ironically bustles off to arrange for Samson's ransom. In his final recognition that "death who sets all free/ Hath paid his ransom now and full discharge" (1572–73) he rises no higher than the pagan conception of death as release from affliction. All these attempts to purify the ideas of bondage and deliverance remain within the limited moral and spiritual vision of paganism and Old Testament Judaism; nowhere is there a realization that because of Adam's sin man is in bondage to Satan and that Christ is his only deliverer, that it is Christ's death alone that sets all men free, and that to the faithful death is "the Gate of Life."

In the same manner the theme of blindness receives at most a moral purification. Manoa characteristically hopes for a miracle, the literal restoration of Samson's sight. The Chorus refers to Samson's "inward eyes" (1689), but they do not suggest that he can tell of things invisible to mortal sight. Samson's insight, like his insight about his bondage to Dalila, is that his present blindness is not so bad as when he "saw not how degenerately [he] serv'd" (419). When we compare Samson's limited awareness with Milton's exalted spiritualizing of blindness in the invocation to Book III of *Paradise Lost,* are we not justified in assuming that Samson suffers a kind of spiritual, as well as physical, blindness?

The contrast between the old dispensation of the letter and the new dispensation of the spirit is deliberately heightened, I suggest, by Milton's technique of putting into the mouths of the characters words that almost automatically call for a metaphorical interpretation by the Christian reader. One of my students saw in the following lines an oblique allusion to the Crucifixion:

> O dark, dark, dark, amid the blaze of noon,
> Irrecoverably dark, total Eclipse
> Without all hope of day!   (80–82)

If that seems too private, more than one commentator has heard Christian overtones in the following lines of Manoa:

> Reject not then what offer'd means, who knows
> But God hath set before us, to return thee
> Home to thy country and his sacred house,   (516–18)

and

>   I however
> Must not omit a Father's timely care
> To prosecute the means of thy deliverance
> By ransom or how else.   (601–4)

The most obvious example is the Chorus's comparison of Samson to the Phoenix:

> So virtue giv'n for lost,
> Deprest, and overthrown, as seem'd,
> Like that self-begott'n bird
> In the *Arabian* woods embost,
> That no second knows nor third,
> And lay erewhile a Holocaust,
> From out her ashy womb now teem'd,
> Revives, reflourishes, then vigorous most

> When most unactive deem'd,
> And though her body die, her fame survives,
> A secular bird ages of lives.   (1697–1707)

The comparison of Christ to the phoenix was a Christian commonplace; here, significantly, the phoenix is not even used as a symbol of personal immortality, but only of the immortality of fame.

Alongside such terms, whose Christian significance provides an ironic counterpoint to the literal significance intended by the speakers, we find words that can only be regarded as Old Testament or pagan. The emphasis on revenge at the end of the play is the notorious example; equally pagan is the Chorus's reliance on the concepts of fortune, chance, and lot in the famous passage on patience already quoted. It is hard to avoid the conclusion that Milton, far from trying to Christianize *Samson Agonistes,* was at some pains to maintain the integrity of his Old Testament materials. Instead of collapsing Samson and Christ, he is concerned to measure the distance between various levels of awareness (represented by Manoa, the Chorus, and Samson) possible to those living under the old dispensation and the level of awareness revealed by Christ in *Paradise Regained.*

In what respect, then, is Milton's Samson like Christ? Did Milton simply turn his back on the whole tradition of Christian exegesis of the Samson story? With much of that tradition he no doubt had little sympathy. One cannot think that Milton regarded the carrying off of the gates of Azzah as a type of the harrowing of Hell; or the jawbone of the ass as a type of the Gospel; or Samson's locks as the rays of heavenly contemplation.

Certainly no such fanciful resemblances found their way into *Samson Agonistes.* In the list of parallels between Samson and Christ given in Thomas Hayne's *The General View of the Holy Scriptures,* however, there is a significant item which, taken in conjunction with Arnold Stein's analysis of the meaning of Samson's *agon,* fully reveals Milton's intention. The last of Hayne's parallels reads (in part) as follows: "Christs Divinitie permitting it, he was bound, led to the Judgement hall, mocked. . . ." In the opposite column: "The spirit of God, which strengthened Sampson, permitting, he was bound, led away, mocked. . . ." [7]

Samson's agonized consciousness that he is an object of scorn and mockery is a motive that runs all through the play. As early as line 34 he complains that he has been made the "scorn and gaze" of his enemies; a little later he says he is exposed

> To daily fraud, contempt, abuse and wrong,
> Within doors, or without, still as a fool,
> In power of others, never in my own.   (76–78)

When he hears the Chorus approaching he thinks it is his enemies "who come to stare/ At my affliction, and perhaps to insult" (112–13), and he reverts to this topic at least twelve more times in the course of the play. The climax of this theme is reached when Samson refuses to go with the Philistine officer:

> Have they not Sword-players, and ev'ry sort
> Of Gymnic Artists, Wrestlers, Riders, Runners,
> Jugglers and Dancers, Antics, Mummers, Mimics,

[7] Thomas Hayne, *The General View of the Holy Scriptures* (London, 1640), p. 218, reproduced in F. Michael Krouse, *Milton's Samson and the Tradition* (Princeton, 1949), facing p. 69.

> But they must pick mee out with shackles tir'd,
> And over-labor'd at thir public Mill,
> To make them sport with blind activity?

> .   .   .

> Can they think me so broken, so debas'd
> With corporal servitude, that my mind ever
> Will condescend to such absurd commands?
> Although thir drudge, to be thir fool or jester,
> And in my midst of sorrow and heart-grief
> To show them feats, and play before thir god,
> The worst of all indignities, yet on me
> Join'd with extreme contempt? I will not come.
>
> (1323-28, 1335-42)

But he does come, and, as Stein so finely says, the man who
has failed as the athlete of God succeeds as the Fool of God.[8]
Is Samson himself conscious of the significance of his new role?
Has he finally learned that it is humiliation that exalts? Earlier
he had acknowledged that the indignities heaped on him by
Harapha were inflicted justly by God; here there is no indication
in the text that Samson attaches any moral or spiritual significance to his willingness to suffer public humiliation at the
Philistine games. On the contrary, he obviously still thinks of
himself as the athlete of God:

> If there be aught of presage in the mind,
> This day will be remarkable in my life
> By some great act, or of my days the last.   (1387-89)

[8] Stein, *Heroic Knowledge*, p. 196.

And it is as act, not as passion, that Manoa and the Chorus regard Samson's victory. He has revenged himself on his enemies and heroically has finished a life heroic. Only in a few words of the Messenger do we get a glimpse of the Samson who might have been:

> He patient but undaunted where they led him,
> Came to the place . . .   (1623–24)

But not to the place called Golgotha. Even in this essential parallel between Samson and Christ we are acutely aware of the difference between the "faithful champion" who destroys his enemies and the Savior who forgives and redeems his.

The harshness of the contrast between Samson's ethic and Christ's may be mitigated by regarding the destruction of the Philistines as a foreshadowing of God's terrible judgment on evil and of the Last Judgment in particular. Such an interpretation, however, robs Samson of his existential reality and makes of the play a ghostly paradigm. If, on the other hand, we view Samson first of all as a concrete individual living in a concrete historical situation, then we must insist that his significance for the Christian reader lies primarily in his inability to measure up to the heroic norm delineated in *Paradise Regained*. For it is humiliation that exalts, not the ruin of a pagan temple. Although he dimly foreshadows the humiliation of his Savior, Samson remains blind to the spiritual significance of his suffering. He cannot know, nor can Manoa and the Chorus, that they must all remain in bondage until the death of One who will in truth, not in shadow, prosecute the means of their deliverance and return them home to their Father's house.

Edward Weismiller

THE "DRY" AND "RUGGED" VERSE

Almost from the beginning of Milton criticism, commentators have felt the dark need to distinguish between the style of *Paradise Lost* (majestic, rich, complex) and the plainer styles of *Paradise Regained* and *Samson Agonistes*. Thus after an admiring analysis of musical patterning in the verse of *Paradise Lost,* John Addington Symonds said:

> Paradise Regained presents a marked change. Except in descriptive passages, there is but little alliterative melody; while all the harsh inversions and rugged eccentricities of abnormally constructed verses are retained. . . . No doubt there are admirers of Milton who would not allow that the metrical changes in Paradise Regained are for the worse. Yet it is hardly to be denied that, in comparison with the Paradise Lost, much of richness, variety, sonorousness, and liquid melody has been sacrificed. Samson Agonistes is a step beyond Paradise Regained in dryness, ruggedness, and uncompromising severity.[1]

[1] John Addington Symonds, "The Blank Verse of Milton," *Fortnightly Review,* New Series, XVI (December, 1874), 780–81.

We had better not, I think, allow to slip past us Symonds'
remark about "the metrical changes in Paradise Regained." For
of course there are none. *Paradise Regained,* like *Paradise Lost,*
is written in *"English* Heroic Verse"; that is, it is written in the
syllabic meter which the principal English poets of the sixteenth
and seventeenth centuries developed—with a greater or lesser
degree of awareness of what they were doing—on the model of
Italian syllabic meter. Milton's early stanzaic verse is, like that
of his contemporaries, also syllabic; and finally, *Samson
Agonistes,* puzzling in effect though it may often be, is composed essentially in the same meter.

Yet it is true that *Paradise Regained* and the *Samson* contain
a large number of lines which are prosodically more difficult
than all but a few lines of *Paradise Lost;* even the blank verse
of *Samson* (the dramatic blank verse that makes up more than
75 percent of the poem) is so written as at times to seem basically
unfamiliar in construction. Doubtless we have today some acci-
dental difficulties in reading—more difficulties than seventeenth-
century readers would have had. We may consider in this light,
for example, *SA* 958,

> *Cherish thy hast'n'd widowhood with the gold
> Of Matrimonial treason: so farewel.[2]

A brash modern might well read

$$\text{Cher-ish} \mid \text{thy hast} \mid \text{'n'd wid} \mid \text{ow-hood} \mid \text{with the gold}$$

---

[2] The text, as in subsequent quotations from *Samson Agonistes,* is that of
1671. Here, as well as elsewhere, I use the asterisk to identify the line specifically
referred to.

and never realize he was in trouble; a more sophisticated reader, persuaded that the line must in fact have been a decasyllable, could hardly feel less than bewilderment. Even if he had encountered dissyllabic "cher'ishing" (i.e., "cher*i*shing," "cher-'shing") in Cowley's *Davideis* (1.809), he would nowhere, so far as I know, have found monosyllabic "cher'ish"; but if "cher*i*sh" *were* possible, *SA* 958 still could not begin with four accentual trochees. Thus seemingly cornered, more editors than one have in dismay "read" dissyllabic "hast'n'd" as a monosyllable.[3] But the pieces of the puzzle fall neatly into place once we have noted, in one of Donne's early verse letters to Mr. Rowland Woodward, the line

Like one who'in her third widdowhood doth professe [4]

—and in the *OED,* the (fifteenth-century) form "wydewood," which the simple and utterly commonplace syncope of medial [ə] will reduce to a dissyllable, the result being a quite possibly stable speech form. Milton's contemporary audience would, I suspect, have read *SA* 958 without difficulty as

Cher-ish | thy hast|'n'd wid'|w'ood with | the gold.

[3] Indeed, "ris'n" is monosyllabic in, e.g., *PL* x.555, "prison" in *PL* vi.660, and "chos'n" in PL 1.318 and iv.691; but "fasten," "hasten," "listen," and their inflected forms seem always dissyllabic in Milton's poetry. And there is some likelihood that Milton still pronounced the *t* in "hasten('d)"; if he did, this would of course have worked against contraction. The *'n* in "hast'n'd" in *SA* 958 is, by the way, a representation of syllabic *n,* not an indication of contraction; cf. dissyllabic "Hast'n," *SA* 576.

[4] The text is as it is given in *John Donne, Complete Poetry and Selected Prose,* ed. John Hayward (Bloomsbury, 1929), p. 156.

But how were they, and how are we, to explain such a line as *Samson* 842,

> Or by evasions thy crime uncoverst more,

without accepting the presence in the line of a trisyllabic foot, or of an extrametrical syllable at a hardly existent caesura—either of which would throw into confusion our understanding of the prosody of the rest of the poem?

In fact, *Samson* 842 is patterned directly upon one possible rhythmic variety of the Italian syllabic line. Petrarch's *Rime Sparse* XXIII, 163 provides a reasonably close parallel:

> sí che 'l foco di Gíove in parte spense.

In Milton we read

> Or by evasions thy crime uncoverst more.

"Or b' evasions" is not perhaps impossible; but it is more likely that we are to allow the initial vowel of "evasions" to blend with and as it were disappear into the vowel of "by," leaving what is in effect an aphaeretic form. Whichever choice we make, we must then read the (resulting) first six syllables of the line at a deliberate pace to prevent them from falling into the meter of English accentual anapestics, a meter which—needless to say—conflicts seriously with that in which the poem was actually written. The situation is in terms of accent the same as that encountered in the last six syllables of *PL* vi.866,

> Burnt after them to the bottomless pit;

it occurs often in Italian verse, increasingly (and obviously not by accident) in Milton's later verse, and relatively infrequently in the verse of other English poets. Milton seems to have become unwilling, in his later years, to do without any possible resource that would lend variety of movement to his syllabic line—even where that variety threatened for a moment his basic meter.

Thus, inadequately, the blank verse of *Samson*. The problems it presents can, I think, be solved; they are fundamentally similar to those raised by the blank verse of *Paradise Lost* and *Paradise Regained*. But they are not, of course, the most serious problems we encounter in the prosodic study of *Samson Agonistes*. The choral verse of that poem is in line after line difficult or uncertain to the ear. And its structure has never yet, so far as I know, been satisfactorily explained.

To remind ourselves of how the choral verse goes, let us read once again *Samson* 1268–1307, the chorus which follows the departure of His Giantship, Harapha of Gath:

> Oh how comely it is and how reviving
> To the Spirits of just men long opprest!
> When God into the hands of thir deliverer
> Puts invincible might
> To quell the mighty of the Earth, th' oppressour,
> The brute and boist'rous force of violent men
> Hardy and industrious to support
> Tyrannic power, but raging to pursue
> The righteous and all such as honour Truth;
> He all thir Ammunition

And feats of War defeats
With plain Heroic magnitude of mind
And celestial vigour arm'd,
Thir Armories and Magazins contemns,
Renders them useless, while
With winged expedition
Swift as the lightning glance he executes
His errand on the wicked, who surpris'd
Lose thir defence distracted and amaz'd.
  But patience is more oft the exercise
Of Saints, the trial of thir fortitude,
Making them each his own Deliverer,
And Victor over all
That tyrannie or fortune can inflict,
Either of these is in thy lot,
Samson, with might endu'd
Above the Sons of men; but sight bereav'd
May chance to number thee with those
Whom Patience finally must crown.
This Idols day hath bin to thee no day of rest,
  Labouring thy mind
More then the working day thy hands,
And yet perhaps more trouble is behind.
For I descry this way
Some other tending, in his hand
A Scepter or quaint staff he bears,
Comes on amain, speed in his look.
By his habit I discern him now

A Public Officer, and now at hand.
His message will be short and voluble.

Now, some of these lines are—there is no question about it—
difficult to know how to read. More than that, they are difficult
to read twice in the same way. For the monodies and choral
odes of the *Samson* are made up of lines ranging in length from
four syllables to twelve; lines of varying length follow one another in no predictable or patterned order. Some of these lines
have feminine endings, and some are acephalous or headless.
Such lines are already removed, at one degree, from the "regular"; if, as they may, they carry unusual accent sequences, they
will seem to us more uncertain in construction still. In a syllabic
meter, however, as long as we can count the syllables of the
lines—and hear the numerical proportioning of one line to another—we cannot wholly lose our way. It follows equally that
the introduction of possible but not mandatory contractions, eli-
sions, or other metrical compressions into syllabic lines already
irregular, lines of uneven and unpredetermined length, leaves
such lines prosodically in a state of nearly absolute uncertainty.

Consider the first line of the passage just quoted,

Oh how | comely | it is and how reviving.

I read the line as beginning with an accentual double trochee,
like *Samson* 175,

Universally crown'd with highest praises.

But in so reading, I reject (in line 1268) a perfectly possible synaloepha or *pronunzia congiunta,* "comely‿it," which is not unlike the compression actually required in *Samson* 1078,

> Though for no friendly‿intent. I am of *Gath*.

If we read

> Oh | how come|ly‿it is | and how | reviv(ing

the line is accentually regular—but acephalous. Well, why should it not be, after all? *Samson* 606 reads

> O | that tor|ment should | not be | confin'd.

But

> Oh | how come|ly‿it is | and how | reviv(ing

has a feminine ending; a "headless" line with a "feminine ending"—why is it not in fact a trochaic pentameter? Presumably we do not look on it so, any more than we call

> Whan | that A|prille with | his shour|es sot(e

a trochaic pentameter. At all events we must not deceive ourselves into supposing that what we "call" the line does not matter. For language is to a considerable degree plastic. No line of poetry is, then, completely independent of our sense of its nature; the way we think of it will determine the way we read.

The second line of the chorus, 1269, I read as beginning—like "Or by evasions thy crime uncoverst more"—with the accentual pyrrhic-trochee-iamb sequence:

$$\overset{x}{\text{To}}\ \overset{x}{\text{the}}\ |\ \overset{/\ x}{\text{Spirits}}\ |\ \overset{x\ /}{\text{of just}}\ |\ \text{men long}\ |\ \text{opprest;}$$

as I have pointed out, Milton uses this accent sequence often in his late poems. But it happens that the word "spirit" is frequently treated as a monosyllable in seventeenth-century English poetry;[5] and if we read "Spirits" so in *Samson* 1269, this line too, shrinking by a syllable, becomes acephalous:

$$\overset{x}{\text{To}}\ |\ \overset{x}{\text{the}}\ \overset{/\frown}{\text{Spirits}}\ |\ \text{of just}\ |\ \text{men\ long}\ |\ \text{opprest.}$$

Such a reading leaves an unaccented syllable standing in the place of the whole first foot of the line—but again, why not? A comparable situation occurs without question a few lines later, in 1280,

> With plain Heroic magnitude of mind
> $$*\overset{x}{\text{And}}\ |\ \text{celes}|\overset{\frown}{\text{tial}}\ \text{vig}|\text{our arm'd.}$$

"Spirits" is monosyllabic in *Samson* 666, dissyllabic in 594. What choice are we to make in line 1269, and on what basis?

And how are we to read 1270,

> When God into the hands of thir deliverer . . . ?

The problem here is with the end of the line, not with the beginning. I read "deliverer" as of three syllables; it is so in at

---

[5] Such rhymes as "sits"–"spirits," Chapman, *Homer's Iliads* XXI.107–8, indicate "sprits" as one common monosyllabic pronunciation of the word in the sixteenth and seventeenth centuries. Another was "sprites"; see, e.g., Helge Kökeritz, *Shakespeare's Pronunciation* (New Haven, 1953), pp. 212–13. Robert Bridges, on the other hand, in *Milton's Prosody* (Oxford, 1921), p. 34, says that "we may be confident" that Milton "suppresses the second vowel, following the Italian."

least three other lines—40, 274, and 1214—of the *Samson*. But in another line still, 279, we must read it as having four syllables. If it has three syllables in *Samson* 1270 the line has five feet and a feminine ending; if it is of four syllables the line becomes a hexameter,

When God | into | the hands | of thir | deliv|erer.

Why not? Line 1297, in the same chorus, is an undoubted hexameter,

This I|dols day | hath bin | to thee | no day | of rest.

The problems in this one chorus do not end here. Are we to read line 1274 as an acephalous pentameter,

Har|dy and | indus|trious to | support,

or as a tetrameter,

Hardy and | indus|trious to | support;

line 1305 as

By | his hab|it I | discern | him now

or as

By his hab|it I | discern | him now . . . ?

Is line 1298 a dimeter,

Labouring | thy mind,

or an acephalous trimeter,

$$\text{La}\overset{/}{|}\text{bouring} \overset{x \; x}{|} \text{thy mind} \dots ?$$

Since "labouring" is dissyllabic in all its other occurrences in Milton's poetry, doubtless we will conclude that it is so in *Samson* 1298, and read the line as of four syllables. In the same way we will bring whatever understanding we have developed of Milton's characteristic rhythms, and of seventeenth-century prosody generally, to the consideration of all the problems the choruses of *Samson* present. And we will find readings for the metrically ambiguous lines, simply because we must. But we shall not thereby solve the ambiguities; or at least we shall not without question solve all of them. For Milton, who could have solved them, who could have prevented their occurrence, did not do so. It must be concluded that they remain by his intention.

Samuel Johnson was, as we should expect, unenthusiastic about the versification of *Samson Agonistes;* it is, he says, "in the dialogue much more smooth and harmonious, than in the parts allotted to the chorus, which are often so harsh and dissonant, as scarce to preserve, whether the lines end with or without rhymes, any appearance of metrical regularity." [6] And the playwright Richard Cumberland, though he undertook a defense of the tragedy against some of Johnson's strictures,[7] could himself find little to approve in the prosody: "There is a harshness in the

[6] *The Rambler,* No. 140 (London, 1752), V, 35.
[7] In *The Observer,* IV, 111 (1785); quoted in the Rev. H. J. Todd's *The Poetical Works of John Milton* (3d ed., London, 1826), IV, 331–36.

metre of his Chorus, which to a certain degree seems to border upon pedantry and affectation; he premises that *the measure is indeed of all sorts,* but I must take leave to observe that it is in some places no measure at all, or such at least as the ear will not patiently endure, nor which any recitation can make harmonious." [8]

Cumberland's revealing assumption is that the harshness of meter he finds in the choruses derives from Milton's "close adherence to the model of the Greek tragedy"; and in this respect, he suggests, "we cannot but lament the fidelity of his imitation." [9] Many writers since Cumberland have assumed that the choruses of *Samson* are, even in their prosody, modeled somehow on classical counterparts. The view culminates perhaps in James Holly Hanford's judgment that "the variations from the iambic pattern are so great" in the choruses "that one is inclined to abandon the attempt to recognize a theoretical conformity to this English pattern and consider them frankly as a reproduction of Greek and Roman rhythms." [10]

Those who hold this position usually hold also that the meters of Greek choral verse were not understood in Milton's time— though Milton "must . . . have seen that the prevailing rhythms were trochaic in the formal sung Choruses." [11] Under this interpretation, then, the meter of the choruses of *Samson* must be thought of as patterned on a model from the first indistinct: it "would be that of the freest form known to the ancients, the

---

[8] Todd, *Poetical Works of Milton,* IV, 331–32.   [9] *Ibid.,* IV, 331.
[10] James Holly Hanford, *A Milton Handbook* (4th ed., New York, 1946), p. 324.
[11] *Ibid.,* p. 325*n.*

logaoedic, which is a trochaic measure with dactyls and other substitutions," [12] and it would admit of—classically inspired— variations even upon that uncertain base.

Since we do not know precisely what Milton made of the meters of Greek choral verse, there is clearly no point in denying that he may have tried in the choruses of *Samson* to suggest, in English verse, some of the rhythmic effects he heard in the choruses of classical tragedy. But it *was* English verse he was writing. The trochaic overlay in the choral odes of *Samson* is, despite Gerard Manley Hopkins' opinion that those odes are "counterpointed throughout," [13] an occasional effect. And it must finally be evident that we could hardly read the choruses at all except in terms of English syllabic meter, the meter used by Milton in all the rest of *Samson,* and in all his other poetry. When S. Ernest Sprott says that "the so-called lyric choruses" of *Samson Agonistes* "are essentially heroic blank verse which has thrown off the bondage of preserving a uniform length of line," [14] then, surely he is in the main right.

Sprott goes on to quote Milton's own brief remarks on the meter of the choral odes in his prefatory note to *Samson Agonistes,* "Of that sort of Dramatic Poem which is call'd Tragedy":

The measure of Verse us'd in the Chorus is of all sorts, call'd by the Greeks *Monostrophic,* or rather *Apolelymenon,* without regard had to *Strophe, Antistrophe* or *Epod,* which were

---

[12] *Ibid.,* pp. 325–26.
[13] See *The Correspondence of Gerard Manley Hopkins and Richard Watson Dixon,* ed. C. C. Abbott (London, 1935), p. 15.
[14] S. Ernest Sprott, *Milton's Art of Prosody* (Oxford, 1953), p. 130.

> a kind of Stanza's fram'd only for the Music, then us'd with
> the Chorus that Sung; not essential to the Poem, and therefore
> not material; or being divided into Stanza's or Pauses, they
> may be call'd *Allæostropha.*

Then, however, having called attention to Milton's "very similar
note to the Ode *Ad Joannem Rousium"* [15] as evidence of the
poet's preference "even when writing Latin" for "this open
form," Sprott says, "Little more need be said, except to comment
on some of the more striking results of the emancipated verse." [16]
But monostrophic verse is not so familiar to us that we need no
explanation of it; the term *Apolelymenon*—"that which has been
released"—is not commonplace. To suggest that a form is "open"
or "free" is not to define the nature of its freedom, nor to fix
the limits within which, still, its effects are communicated. At
the very least, if sources for, or illuminating parallels to, Milton's
practice in the writing of the choral odes of *Samson* can be
found in earlier verse, we must attempt to find them.

In his excellent chapter on "The Choruses of *Samson Agonistes"* in *The Italian Element in Milton's Verse,*[17] F. T. Prince
places the choruses "in relation to certain Italian examples, as well
as in relation to Milton's own development or adaptation of the
Italian heroic manner." [18] Prince points out similarities in the
technique of handling the chorus between Milton's *Samson*
and Tasso's *Aminta,* Guarini's *Il Pastor Fido,* and Andreini's

---

[15] *Ibid.,* p. 131*n.*   [16] *Ibid.,* p. 131.
[17] F. T. Prince, *The Italian Element in Milton's Verse* (Oxford, 1954), pp.
145–68.
[18] *Ibid.,* p. 146.

L'Adamo; in particular, he notes the increasing appearance, in sixteenth-century Italian dramatic works which Milton probably knew, of choral odes which are "monostrophic" in Milton's sense of the term (written, that is, in continuously developing, non-repeating forms), and the use by some Italian dramatists of "intermittent rhyme in semi-lyrical dialogues." [19]

Prince also notes the range of line length—from four syllables to twelve—in the stanza Spenser invented for the November eclogue of *The Shepheardes Calender,* and points out Milton's indebtedness to Spenser in his own early and experimental verse. Finally, and most interestingly, Prince analyzes the ways in which unrhymed verse like that of *Samson*'s choruses may—in its "emancipation"—retain some of the formal attributes of rhymed verse. Prince's discussion is worth reading in full; it constitutes a major addition to our understanding of Milton's practice in the writing of the choruses of *Samson Agonistes.* Even so, its three and its one do not, at last, add up to a fully satisfactory four.

Prince himself points out that the "monostrophic" choruses of sixteenth-century Italian drama are—like *canzoni*—written entirely or almost entirely in rhythmically varied but still metrically regular lines of two lengths only: the traditional hendecasyllable and heptasyllable.[20] In the "monostrophic" choruses these lines are freely arranged. And undoubtedly that fact is important for our understanding of the relatively free structure of the monody *Lycidas,* in the *allæostropha* of which a few six-syllable lines (one, line 95, actually a heptasyllable, "They knew not of his

[19] *Ibid.,* pp. 154–55.   [20] *Ibid.,* pp. 158 ff.

story") are interspersed among the prevailing decasyllables. It is tempting to explain lines 80 to 105 of the prologos of *Samson,* with their beautifully formal, yet unexpected, combination of ten- and six-syllable lines, on much the same basis. Still the effect of *Samson* 80–105 is very different from that of, say, 115–75, the entering chorus; and the choruses generally are very different in effect also from English verse in which stanzaic patterns, however elaborate, are established and then repeated.

Let us recognize that though Milton did not intend *Samson Agonistes* to be staged, and did not intend its choral odes to be sung, he must have distinguished clearly between the ode and other poetic forms. He knew the odes of Pindar; he knew the choral odes of Greek drama, the variety and occasional roughness of Greek choral rhythms, and he was familiar with the "monostrophic" odes of Aeschylus. We may accept the suggestion that he had found in Italian drama impressive examples of the "monostrophic" choral ode which showed intermittent rhyme. As for variety of line length, the tradition of English stanzaic verse itself—including, of course, Milton's own *Nativity Ode*—had produced effects of extraordinary beauty and complexity through patterned variation in length of line. In addition, however, Milton had in his young manhood written two irregular, "monostrophic" rhymed odes in English, *On Time* and *At a Solemn Music.* Perhaps it would be appropriate now to glance briefly at the early poems and, indeed, to compare a few lines from them with lines from the late choruses.

Such a comparison reveals at once that Milton used in his earliest poems acephalous or headless lines in which a weakly stressed (or unstressed) syllable must occupy the place of the entire first foot; there are, indeed, some thirty-six such lines in *L'Allegro* and *Il Penseroso* alone, and it is not uninteresting to read such a line as *Samson* 1280,

> And celestial vigour arm'd,

side by side with, e.g., *L'Allegro* 94,

> And the jocond rebecks sound.[21]

It is more interesting still to note that, whether an acephalous line in the early poems begins with a weak or with a strong syllable, the free, unpatterned intermixture of such lines with their fully syllabled counterparts must at times leave us uncertain whether a given line is acephalous or full. Thus in *L'Allegro* 77,

> Towers, and Battlements it sees,

"Towers" may, clearly, be monosyllabic *or* dissyllabic; one may, that is, read "Towrs" or "Towers," and the fact that the spelling is "Towers" is not conclusive. We may wonder too at the construction of such lines as *Comus* 139,

> The nice Morn on th'*Indian* steep,

and *Psalm VII* 45,

> If th'unjust will not forbear,

much as we may wonder at the construction of *Samson* 1700,

---

[21] In quoting from Milton's minor poems I use where possible the 1645 text; otherwise that of 1673.

> In the *Arabian* woods embost.

In all these lines, acceptance of the spelling given in the earliest texts will yield one kind of perfectly acceptable rhythm, rejection of it another; and the most careful study of alternatives, indeed of all pertinent considerations, will not lead us to certainty.[22]

But of all the lines in Milton's early poems, the most interesting to examine in relation to the meter of the choral passages of *Samson Agonistes* is line 12 of the irregular ode *On Time,* taken together with the lines preceding it:

> Which is no more then what is false and vain,
> And meerly mortal dross;
> So little is our loss,
> So little is thy gain.
> For when as each thing bad thou hast entomb'd,
> And last of all, thy greedy self consum'd,
> Then long Eternity shall greet our bliss
> *With an individual kiss.

Now, the single strophe of *On Time* is at the beginning (and at the end) very closely related to Spenser's *Epithalamion* stanza, and this in turn derives in great part from the Italian *canzone*. It is difficult, therefore, not to read *On Time* 12, in context, *as a trimeter,*

---

[22] Bridges, in *Milton's Prosody,* pp. 52–54, notes the ambiguity in structure of certain lines in *L'Allegro* and *Il Penseroso,* and on pp. 53–55 associates it loosely with structural ambiguity in the choral verse of *Samson Agonistes.* But his conclusions as they relate to the *Samson* seem to me almost completely disappointing—in part wrong, in part vague or superficial. My general debt to Bridges—like that of every other historical prosodist in this century—is nonetheless, of course, unreckonably large.

With an in|divid|ūal kiss—

a trimeter with, it is true, an oddly exceptional first foot, exceptional once again because trisyllabic feet hardly occur elsewhere
in Milton. In fact, *On Time* 12 is an acephalous tetrameter. We
have no difficulty in recognizing as such the closely similar line
Comus 973,

With | a crown | of death|less Praise,

simply because the tetrameter context operates to give us absolute
assurance:

And sent them here through hard assays
*With a crown of deathless Praise.

But in the twenty-two lines of *On Time,* the single full tetrameter occurs *later* in the poem, at line 20, and there is no other
acephalous line.

And from this it must be clear why, though we may find in
Milton's early poems lines displaying almost all the rhythmic
variety of lines later to be found in *Samson Agonistes,* this fact
does not quite prepare us for a reading of the choruses of *Samson:* for most of Milton's early poetry provides a reasonably firm
metrical context for its "difficult" lines, thereby minimizing their
difficulty, whereas most of the difficult lines in *Samson Agonistes*
are ambiguous in structure precisely for the reason that *On Time*
12 is ambiguous—because the metrical context gives us uncertain,
even conflicting, directions for reading. The firm fact must be
repeated: Milton cannot have failed to recognize the uncertain

condition of these lines; he could have eliminated it and did not do so. We must look further for an explanation of the use of such lines—with all their difficulty, and all their metrical interest.

Apart from actual ambiguity of structure in some of the lines of *Samson*'s choral odes, the strangeness of rhythmical effect in those odes arises principally from the fact that, in them, lines of differing length occur together in combinations to which the ear trained in the rhythms of English stanzaic poetry is little accustomed. We may take as an example the ordinary use of the twelve-syllable line, the English hexameter or Alexandrine, in sixteenth- and seventeenth-century verse. Noting that a twelve-syllable line *begins* the stanza in the November eclogue of Spenser's *Shepheardes Calender,* Prince does not point out how unusual it is that this should be so.[23] Much more familiar to us is the use of the Alexandrine to close and cap, as it were, the *Faerie Queene* stanza. There are fifty twelve-syllable lines in the early poetry of Milton himself; and what we may not realize without examining that poetry is that every one of these occurs as the final line of a stanza or as the final line of a poem. In his early work, therefore, Milton like virtually all of his fellow poets (including Donne) uses the hexameter to bring a formal rhyme pattern *and a grammatical utterance* to a full and rounded close. Of the thirty hexameters in *Samson Agonistes,* on the other hand, not one concludes a choral ode, or even a section of a choral ode; three are followed by semicolons and five by periods or exclamation marks, but the rest occur in mid-sentence as in mid-paragraph, and many of them are strongly enjambed or run

---

[23] Prince, *Italian Element,* pp. 163–64.

on, closely tied in every way, therefore, to following lines of a variety of differing lengths. The effect is radically unfamiliar to our ears.

Similar comments could be made on Milton's use, in *Samson Agonistes,* of the seven-syllable line, the acephalous tetrameter. This line had been used, in English poetry, as the occasional variant-equivalent of the full octosyllable (or iambic tetrameter) since the thirteenth century; in Chaucer we find it so used in the *Romaunt of the Rose* (at, e.g., line 133), in the *Book of the Duchesse* (line 5), and in the *Hous of Fame* (line 40, etc.)—and with a presumed feminine ending, so that it counterfeits a full trochaic tetrameter, in such a line as *Hous of Fame* 35,

> Causeth swiche dremes ofte.

The tetrameter with its variants continued to be much employed after the time of Chaucer; and Milton, whether or not he was acquainted with all its long history, must have been familiar with the acephalous tetrameter as a staple of Elizabethan lyric. In his early verse over three hundred such lines occur. But they occur there, as they occur in the poetry of his predecessors, all but invariably in a context of full tetrameters, and thus are heard as tetrameters. In *Samson Agonistes,* on the other hand, except in the highly formal, rhymed, final choruses, they are preceded and followed most often by lines of ten, twelve, six, four, and nine syllables. The rhythmic strangeness of *SA* 607,

> O that torment should not be confin'd
> *To the bodies wounds and sores,

is for this reason far greater than that of any acephalous line or lines in *L'Allegro* or *Il Penseroso*. Again we must assume that the strangeness is intended; but we do well to recognize it as a strangeness produced in the first place by a kind of controlled metrical-rhythmical disorientation, and persisting as a strangeness of proportioning—a complex effect for which the reading of stanzaic verse, even Milton's own stanzaic verse, has hardly prepared us.

There remain *On Time* and *At a Solemn Music*. In *Apollo and the Nine,* Carol Maddison credits Milton with having been the first poet to write, in these poems, irregular odes in English.[24] Miss Maddison suggests that, in doing so, he was following the lead of neolatin poets who, improvising perhaps on the basis of "verse samplers" written in the sixteenth century by Julius Caesar Scaliger to illustrate (in combination) all the classical meters known, produced a variety of "mixed odes," false dithyrambs, and poems in free verse.[25] The mixed ode consisted "of a mixture of various classical stanzas or of metrical units normally used only by themselves in homogeneous wholes"; [26] all three forms were unconventional and experimental. In the late sixteenth and the seventeenth century, exercises were set at the universities in the writing of irregular Latin verse, and these, Miss Maddison believes, "suggested to English poets the writing of irregular verse in English." [27] She mentions Milton's Latin ode to John Rouse— not, of course, a university exercise, but a poem in the tradition of the irregular Latin ode—as being "composed of unfamiliar

---

[24] Carol Maddison, *Apollo and the Nine* (London, 1960), p. 330.
[25] *Ibid.,* pp. 330–36.   [26] *Ibid.,* p. 332.   [27] *Ibid.,* p. 336.

combinations of Latin verses."[28] She does not note that Milton's early irregular odes in English are, except at one or two difficult points, irregular rather in being "monostrophic" than in displaying combinations of English syllabic lines not ordinarily found together.

Poems of Mr. John Milton, in which *On Time* and *At a Solemn Music* were first published, appeared in 1645; the ode *Ad Ioannem Rousium,* though it was not published until 1673, was written in 1646. In 1646 was published *Steps to the Temple,* a collection of religious poems by Richard Crashaw, bound together with a group of secular poems, *The Delights of the Muses.* In the latter we find Crashaw writing Latin dithyrambs and free verse; and in the English poems of *Steps to the Temple* he employs not merely the acephalous tetrameter, as, we have seen, many poets had done before him, but the acephalous trimeter, as Milton had done here and there in the *Nativity Ode*—and, quite extraordinarily, uses both together, as Milton had done in the second and third songs of *Arcades.*

> Such a rural Queen
> All *Arcadia* hath not seen

writes Milton, and Crashaw, in, e.g. 14.1–4 of *The Weeper,*

> Golden though hee bee,
> Golden *Tagus* murmurs though,
> Might he flow from thee,
> Content and quiet would he goe.[29]

[28] *Ibid.,* p. 333.
[29] Crashaw's text is as it is given in *The Poems English Latin and Greek of Richard Crashaw,* ed. L. C. Martin (Oxford, 1927), p. 81.

The sensibility that informs *The Weeper* is profoundly unlike Milton's; and yet the careful reader of Crashaw's poem is, I think, bound to hear in it, and in the irregular English verse of such a poem as *On a prayer booke sent to Mrs. M.R.,* some cadences he would not have expected to hear outside the 1645 *Poems.* A second edition of *Steps to the Temple,* containing English verse more irregular still, and still more expertly written, appeared in 1648; in 1649 Crashaw died.

It is possible that Milton and Crashaw knew or knew of one another; it is by no means impossible that they affected one another's writing. It is certain that Crashaw and Abraham Cowley knew one another well. In 1647 Cowley published *The Mistress;* in 1656 he published a much enlarged *Poems,* in which volume were included a number of "Pindarique Odes, Written in Imitation of the Stile and Maner of the Odes of Pindar." About the meter of the originals from which he worked or drew his inspiration, Cowley says, "We must consider that our Ears are strangers to the Musick of . . . [Pindar's] *Numbers* . . . for though the *Grammarians* and *Criticks* have laboured to reduce his Verses into regular feet and measures . . . yet in effect they are little better than *Prose* to our Ears." [30] For this reason, among others, Cowley does not attempt a literal translation of Pindar; he makes it his aim not so much "to let the Reader know precisely what he spoke, as what was his *way* and *manner* of speaking; which has not been yet (that I know of) introduced into *English,* though it be the noblest and highest kind of writing in

---

[30] Abraham Cowley, *Poems* (London, 1656), sig. Aaa2ʳ. In quoting from the *Odes* themselves I use the 1656 text where possible; otherwise that given in *The Works of Mʳ Abraham Cowley* (London, 1668).

Verse. . . . This *Essay* is but to try how it will look in an *English habit."* [31]

The "way and manner of speaking," by which Cowley means style in its largest sense, must not be confused with the "English habit," which is irregular verse. For centuries Cowley was credited unreservedly with having invented the form of English "Pindaric" verse: "Every one knows it was introduc'd into our Language, in this Age, by the happy Genius of Mr. *Cowley"*—the comment is Dryden's, in the preface to *Sylvae.*[32] Critics of the present century are for the most part agreed that Cowley received this poetic instrument at the hands of Crashaw; George N. Shuster even suggests that it may have been Crashaw—noted as a Greek scholar—who brought Pindar to Cowley's attention.[33] All this may well be so. Still it must be insisted that if there are many cadences to be found in the *Pindarique Odes* which remind us of Crashaw—and some few which could remind us of Milton's early odes—there are also many cadences which are new. The instrument, in Cowley's hands, is very much developed. In the *Pindarique Odes* we find English syllabic lines *in most of the extraordinary variety of different lengths and sequences in which they are to be found, later, in the choral odes of* Samson Agonistes.

Cowley's *Odes,* like Milton's choral odes, are allæostrophic; that is, they give the effect of formal design, but repeat no stanzaic or strophic pattern. On the other hand, in all the "Pindarique" odes which Cowley wrote up to the time of his death—and he

[31] Cowley, *Poems,* sig. Aaa2ᵛ.

[32] *Miscellany Poems* (London, 1685), II, a7ʳ.

[33] George N. Shuster, *The English Ode from Milton to Keats* (New York, 1940), p. 99.

wrote twenty-nine, totaling over three thousand lines—there are only a very few unrhymed verses; and since the effect of rhyme is strong and characteristic, we must not expect to hear in Cowley's "Pindariques," at every turn, the exact music of the choruses of *Samson,* which are only in small part rhymed. Indeed, Cowley rhymes, most often, adjacent verses; only very occasionally does he use feminine endings; lines are usually end-stopped; and sentences and rhyme structures usually come to a close together. In spite of all this, and allowing for great differences between Cowley and Milton in diction, tone, and (for the most part) subject matter, effects in the *Odes* of odd yet beautiful proportioning in progressions through a series of lines of unpredetermined length must again and again strike our ears as carrying a music more like that of the choruses of *Samson* than like any other we have heard. Here are lines 1–9 from strophe 3 of the *The Resurrection:*

> Whom *Thunders* dismall noise,
> And all that *Prophets* and *Apostles* louder spake,
> And all the *Creatures* plain *conspiring voyce,*
> Could not whilst they *liv'ed,* awake,
> This mightier sound shall make
> When *Dead* t'arise,
> And open *Tombs,* and open *Eyes*
> To the long *Sluggards* of five thousand years.
> This *mightier Sound* shall *make* its *Hearers Ears.*

Here is *The Complaint,* strophe 8, lines 16–19:

> However, of all Princes thou
> Shouldst not reproach Rewards for being small or slow;

Thou who rewardest but with popular breath,
>   And that too after death.

In Crashaw's irregular verse hexameters are rare; there are
310 certain hexameters scattered through the *Pindarique Odes.*
Often they begin, or fall within, sentences, as Milton's were to do
in *Samson Agonistes,* and many of them are rhythmically as complex as any to be found in Milton's poetry:

>   'Tis true, the *two Immortal Syllables* remain,
>   But, Oh ye learned men, explain,
>   What *Essence,* what *Existence* this,
>   What *Substance,* what *Subsistence,* what *Hypostasis*
>   In *Six poor Letters* is?
>   (*Life and Fame,* 3.5–9)

Cowley uses the difficult acephalous tetrameter sometimes safe-
guarded by the full tetrameter, but as often out of its normal
metrical context; and he uses it with great authority:

>   To thee, O *Proserpine,* this *Isle* I give,
>   Said *Jove,* and as he said,
>   Smil'd, and bent his gracious *Head.*
>   (*First Nemeæan Ode of Pindar* 3.1–3)

>   The *Lyon* then shall to the *Leopard* say,
>   *Brother Leopard* come away;
>   Behold a Land which God has giv'en us in prey!
>   (*The 34 Chapter of the Prophet Isaiah* 5.8–10) [34]

[34] The apostrophe in "giv'en," a misprint in the 1656 ed., is in 1668 also; normally in Cowley's usage it would indicate contraction, but in *Isaiah* 5.10 "given" is
(rather unusually for the seventeenth century) a metrical dissyllable.

There are eighty-seven acephalous tetrameters in the *Odes;* many of them begin, as do many of Milton's, with weak syllables. We may compare

> Then long Eternity shall greet our bliss
> With an individual kiss   (*On Time* 11–12)

with these lines of Cowley's:

> Nor is fair *Virtues Picture* seen aright
>   But in *Fortunes* golden light.
>   (*Second Olympique Ode of Pindar* 6.6–7)

As in the choruses of *Samson Agonistes,* it is precisely the variability of line length in Cowley's *Odes* which makes us at times unsure whether to read a possible metrical compression. There is no difficulty with such lines as

> To his Souls true and peaceful Count'ry‿above.
>   (*Upon the Death of the Earl of Balcarres* 3.12)

> Enjoy then all thy‿*afflictions* now.
>   (*Upon His Majesties Restoration and Return* 12.10)

But the situation is far different in, e.g.,

> Ought to be *entail'd* by right of *Birth.*
>   (*Restoration* 8.25)

The line is probably a tetrameter (be *'ntail'd?* b' *entail'd?*), simply because there is no other certain acephalous pentameter in Cowley's *Odes*. But

> Ought | to be | *entail'd* | by right | of *Birth*

remains possible. And similarly, I see no way of determining absolutely the metrical state of the third line of the following passage:

> Each rich embroidered *Line,*
> Which their triumphant *Brows* around,
> By his sacred Hand is bound,
> Does all their *starry Diadems* outshine.
>
> (*The Praise of Pindar* 2.9–12)

"By *his* sacred Hand is bound. . . ." "By *his* habit I discern him now . . ." (*SA* 1305). Such parallels show us both poets in a sense "mixing meters": not precisely as meters were mixed in neolatin irregular verse, certainly, but as boldly as meters can be mixed in English syllabic verse without inviting total breakdown.

It is never possible to isolate rhythms from their context; such similarities as may be heard in the passages just quoted are necessarily, then, both incomplete and transitory. Yet they are very real; and many more examples could be given. Cowley even deliberately disrupts rhythms at times, as Milton was later to do:

> Like fearful *Troops* in some strong *Ambush* ta'ne,
> Shall some fly routed, and some fall slaine,
> Thick as ripe *Fruit,* or yellow *Leaves* in *Autumn* fall.
>
> (*Isaiah* 3.18–20)

> Old *Manoah:* advise
> Forthwith how thou oughtst to receive him.
>
> (*SA* 328–29)

The rhythms in these two passages are not, of course, the same; but disruption of rhythm functions in them in much the same way. Roughness in Cowley's verse sounds occasionally very much like the often-criticized roughness in Donne; and if this observation suggests to us in turn that Milton's mature poetry may be technically somewhat indebted to Donne's, we ought not, I think, dismiss the possibility.

Indeed I have no wish to imply that the source of Milton's verse technique in the choruses of *Samson Agonistes* is anything less than one sum of elements of a vast poetic experience. The irregular verse of *Psalm III*, for example—one of the eight psalms which Milton translated in 1653—itself looks forward to certain effects in the choruses of *Samson*, and presumably independently of Cowley. That the *Pindarique Odes* influenced Milton strongly, on the other hand, is hardly to be doubted. We have the testimony of Milton's third wife for the fact that Cowley ranked with Spenser and Shakespeare as one of Milton's favorite poets.[35] But the principal evidence for a connection between the *Pindarique Odes* and the choruses of *Samson Agonistes* is to be gathered, all but explicitly, from the writings of Milton's nephew Edward Phillips.

Phillips, in his youth tutored by Milton, continued during his adult life to seek his famous uncle's company—paid him "frequent visits to the last," as Phillips himself says;[36] served him from time to time as reader and amanuensis; and discussed with him, obviously, matters of mutual interest and concern: literary matters among others. It follows that Phillips' literary pronounce-

---

[35] See John Milton French, *The Life Records of John Milton* (New Brunswick, N.J., 1949–58), V, 322–23.

[36] *Ibid.*, V, 70.

ments may well be worth our attention. Here in particular is a passage from the preface to Phillips' *Theatrum Poetarum* (published in 1675, but licensed for printing almost two months before Milton's death in 1674) which should be of great interest to students of *Samson Agonistes:*

> To the Antient Greecs and Latins, the Modern Poets of all Nations and for several Ages, have acknowledged themselves beholding, for those both Precepts and examples which have been thought conducing to the perfection of Poetry; for the manner of its Garb and dress, which is Vers, we in particular to the *Italians*, the first of the Moderns that have been eminently Famous in this Faculty, *the Measure of the Greec and Latin Verse being no way suitable to the Modern Languages* [italics mine]; & truly so far as I have observed the Italian *Stanza* in Heroic Poem, and the Sonnet, Canzon, and Madrigal in the Lyric, as they have been formerly more frequently made use of by the *English* than by any, so except their own proper Language they become none better then ours.[37]

"There is certainly a decency in one sort of Verse more then another which custom cannot really alter," Phillips goes on to say;[38] and this propriety he finds especially, for English lyric verse, in the form of

> the *Italian* Sonnet and Canzon, above *Pindaric* Ode, which, whatever the name pretends, comes not so near in resemblance to the Odes of *Pindarus,* as the Canzon, which though it answers not so exactly as to consist of *Stroph, Antistroph* and

[37] Edward Phillips, *Theatrum Poetarum* (London, 1675), sigs. **3ʳ⁻ᵛ.
[38] *Ibid.,* sig. **3ᵛ.

Epod, yet the Verses, which in the first *Stroph* of the Canzon were tied to no fixt number, order or measure, nevertheless in the following Srophs [*sic*] return in the same number, order & measure, as were observ'd in the first; whereas that which we call the *Pindaric,* hath a nearer affinity with the *Monostrophic,* or *Apolelymenon,* used in the Chorus's of *Æschylus* his Tragedies.[39]

Let us return for a moment to Milton's prefatory note to *Samson Agonistes.* "The measure of Verse us'd in the Chorus is of all sorts, call'd by the Greeks *Monostrophic,* or rather *Apolelymenon,* without regard had to *Strophe, Antistrophe* or *Epod."*

If there were no more similarity between Milton's note and Phillips' introduction to the *Theatrum Poetarum* than has just been illustrated, their congruence would be striking enough. Later in his preface, however, Phillips speaks (for our purposes) more illuminatingly still. He is unwilling, as we have just seen, that Pindaric verse should drive out of English all other kinds of lyric measure; but this does not mean that he finds the Pindaric unsuitable for all possible poetic uses. Speaking of tragedy, he says,

As for the *Ethos* . . . I shall only leave it to consideration whether the use of the *Chorus,* and the observation of the ancient Law of Tragedy, particularly as to limitation of time, would not rather by reviving the pristine glory of the *Tragic* [*p*]*all,* advance then diminish the present . . . and for the Verse if it must needs be Rime, I am clearly of opinion that way of

[39] *Ibid.,* sig. **4[r].

Versifying, which bears the name of *Pindaric,* and which hath
no necessity of being divided into *Strophs* or *Stanzas* would
be much more suitable for *Tragedy* then the continued *Rhapsodie* of Riming Couplets.[40]

Phillips echoes sentiments and even phrases of Milton's in the
two passages quoted, and in their contexts; he echoes very
closely, for example, Milton's disapproving remarks about the
"error of intermixing Comic stuff with Tragic sadness and
gravity." [41] One need not claim (what has never been demon-
trated) that Milton himself wrote, or revised, or contributed
directly to the Preface or any other part of *Theatrum Poetarum*
in order to find significance in this.[42] What is particularly revealing is, of course, Phillips' firm association of English Pindaric
verse with monostrophic verse—"or *Apolelymenon*"—and the
suggestion that such verse is especially suitable for tragedy; in
which the use of the Chorus is recommended. The example Phillips had before him we know.[43] And though the Pindaric element

---

[40] *Ibid.,* sigs. **8^{r-v}. There is in all copies I have examined a considerable space
between *"Tragic"* and *"all";* and on sig. B4^{v} Aeschylus is said to have been
"mention'd by *Horace* as the first bringer up of the Tragic pall." See also *Il Penseroso* 97–98. But the intended reading may nonetheless have been, of course,
simply "the *Tragicall,*" i.e., the tragic.

[41] *Ibid.,* sig. **8^{r}.

[42] Such claims have, however, often been made; see, e.g., Walter Harte, *The
Amaranth* (London, 1767), p. 234$n;$ and cf. French, *Life Records of Milton,* V, 71.

[43] Why did he not identify it explicitly? Perhaps the answer is to be found in
the notice of Milton which appears later in *Theatrum Poetarum* (sigs. Ee 9^{r-v}).
Phillips speaks of Milton very briefly, as "the Author . . . of two Heroic Poems,
and a Tragedy; namely *Paradice lost, Paradice Regain'd,* and *Sampson Agonista;*
in which how far he hath reviv'd the Majesty and true *Decorum* of Heroic Poesy
and Tragedy: it will better become a person less related then my self, to deliver
his judgement."

in *Samson* does not contain, proportionately, a great deal of rhyme, such rhyme as it does contain is, in fact, much like Cowley's in the *Odes*. At any rate it is not "the continued *Rhapsodie* of Riming Couplets."

Elsewhere in the *Theatrum Poetarum* Phillips speaks at length of Cowley, calling him "the most applauded Poet of our Nation both of the present and past Ages," and attaching his name to the invention of Pindaric verse in English.[44] Doubtless Milton was more fully conscious than Phillips of the many elements that had gone into the English Pindaric tradition. This need not keep us from recognizing that in the *Theatrum Poetarum* there is established a very direct, even decisive, connection between the choruses of *Samson* and Cowley's *Pindarique Odes*.

But even as one affirms the relationship, one wishes to reaffirm the independence of *Samson Agonistes,* its ultimate dissimilarity to, or advance beyond, anything that preceded it in English. There is extraordinary rhythmic variety in Cowley; but in the approximately 275 trimeters which the *Pindarique Odes* contain, there are no lines remotely like, e.g., *SA* 298 and 618,

> But the heart of the Fool.
>
> As a lingring disease.

These lines are precisely related to *SA* 842,

> Or by evasions thy crime uncoverst more,

and a formal source for their accentual pattern is to be found, as might be anticipated, in one accentual variety of the Italian

⁴⁴ *Ibid.*, sigs. Aaʳ· ᵛ.

*hepta*syllable. See again, for example, Petrarch's *Rime Sparse,* this time L, lines 35, 36, 69, and 72, the latter two of which read

$$
\begin{array}{ccccccc}
x & x & / & x & x & / & x \\
\end{array}
$$
a chi tutto diparte

and

$$
\begin{array}{ccccccc}
x & x & / & x & x & / & x \\
\end{array}
$$
dal matino⌣a la sera.

And with this observation we may come to a final summary analysis of Milton's metrical practice in the choral odes of *Samson Agonistes*. Each line in the odes is a syllabic line, its form derived from some part of the English tradition, or (less often) directly from the Italian tradition, on the basis of which, as Edward Phillips affirms, English syllabic verse was developed. But syllabic lines are, in the choruses of *Samson,* "mixed": not because they do not in fact belong ultimately to one basic meter, or to meters basically allied, but because the sequences in which they appear in *Samson* often set up unusual proportions and unusual rhythms, and because a few uncommon lines are here and there deliberately used without the contextual safeguards which, in the verse that supplies their pattern, tend to make their construction immediately understandable.

Milton's practice, significantly like Cowley's in many respects, differs from Cowley's in that Milton does not use in *Samson Agonistes* so great a variety of line lengths as does Cowley in the *Odes;* characteristically, on the other hand, Milton relies more heavily than does his contemporary upon the resources of Italian versification. Again characteristically, this latter difference extends even to Milton's use—or rather, to his general avoidance—of rhyme. We must recall the intermittent rhyme of some of the Italian "monostrophic" choral odes—and think then of the odes of *Samson* as written, perhaps, in that ultimate form of seventeenth-century English irregular verse, the blank or near-blank Italianate Pindaric. The term "Pindaric" as applied to the irregular verse of the *Samson* must, however, be understood to have a prosodic relevance only.

The rhythmic and metrical difficulty of Milton's late irregular verse is undeniable. But in reading *Samson Agonistes* we may well come to feel that even its ambiguities of form, with the tension they produce, the deliberate artifices the reader must employ in the reading to resolve them in favor of the basic meter, have become for Milton a powerful heightening device. We are not to forget "Decorum . . . which is the grand master-piece to observe." [45] And in metrical complexity Milton found, it may be thought, a means more appropriate to the speeches of tragedy than marked rhetorical or musical elaboration would be to keep language which must in itself seem consonant with that of prose from sounding in fact too much like prose.

We have noted Dr. Johnson's opinion of the verse of *Samson Agonistes;* we may note finally his opinion of "the Pindarick style." In the *Life of Cowley* Johnson says,

To the disproportion and incongruity of Cowley's sentiments must be added the uncertainty and looseness of his measures. . . . It is urged by Dr. Sprat, that the *irregularity of numbers is the very thing* which makes *that kind of poesy fit for all*

[45] "Of Education," *The Works of John Milton* (New York, 1931–38), IV, 286.

manner of subjects. But he should have remembered, that what is fit for every thing can fit nothing well. The great pleasure of verse arises from the known measure of the lines, and uniform structure of the stanzas, by which the voice is regulated, and the memory relieved.[46]

And many pages later:

[Cowley's] versification seems to have had very little of his care; and if what he thinks be true, that his numbers are unmusical only when they are ill read, the art of reading them is at present lost; for they are commonly harsh to modern ears.[47]

How familiar it all sounds. And how much indeed was lost, how long ago. With the Restoration, French syllabic verse succeeded Italian as the model for English verse, and much of the difference we now hear between Dryden and Pope on the one hand, and Milton—and Cowley—on the other, resides in that fact. It was a fact which, curiously enough, even the eighteenth century did not know—or of the implications of which eighteenth-century critics were not fully aware. There was then much in Milton (and in Cowley) that Dr. Johnson simply could not hear.

There is much in both poets we ourselves have not been able to hear. The choruses of *Samson* must, I think, go on seeming to us artificial in their prosody; but what verse is not artificial? It is at all events artifice not understood which "seems to border upon pedantry and affectation." As, then, we commence to re-

[46] *The Lives of the English Poets* (3 vols., Dublin, 1779), I, 55–56.
[47] *Ibid.*, I, 71.

capture an understanding of a phenomenon of English literary history so long obscured, we will also perhaps begin to recapture "the art of reading" Pindaric verse—even Milton's Pindaric verse. And perhaps by and by—who knows?—the verse of *Samson Agonistes* will not seem so dry, so harsh, so rugged, as it has seemed to most readers in the past.

Joseph H. Summers

THE MOVEMENTS OF THE DRAMA

In *Paradise Lost* Milton created and celebrated those movements of falling and rising—of perfection, conflict, destruction, and a new and higher creation—which imaged an entire vision of human life; and the poem ended with Adam and Eve, now fully human, beginning life and history as we know it. In *Paradise Regained* everyone is waiting; the movement of the poem is almost entirely—and formidably—intellectual. We feel continually the impulse toward action and then the countermovement of withdrawal (restraint, patience, or, for Satan, frustration). Only after the exploration of all the wrong ends and means which Satan's temptations provide is the Son's way of action defined by what has been excluded; and the poem, that prelude to action, ends with the promise of a beginning: "Now enter, and begin to save mankind." For *Samson Agonistes* neither of these patterns is irrelevant (there are significant echoes of and analogies to both poems), but neither is adequately descriptive of the major movements. This poem begins with a character in a fallen world who has seemingly already lost everything; for him the problem is not to retain or discover the perfection which is around or within him, nor merely to regain a visionary faith in future possibilities and God's providence. He must recover lost strength and a sense of purpose, and he must achieve a wisdom and a "perfection" which he has never known. He must fulfill his heroic destiny, both his triumph and his death, not in a still indefinite future, but in a few hours. For such an action, Milton abandoned the narrative voice of the epic and the brief epic (or meditative debate) and chose for its embodiment the dramatic form of Greek tragedy.

We should not be disturbed by the fact that we have a tragedy which begins with degradation of the hero and ends with his triumph. (If we have previously decided that no true "tragedy" can provide a metaphysical consolation, we are free to invent another term; but it seems unlikely that a new word will help us much with the realities of the drama.) Nor, if we know Milton's other work, should we be surprised that he chose to imitate what he considered the best Greek models when he wished to give formal embodiment to his Hebraic subject and Christian vision. It is obvious that Milton did not see the conflicts between the Greek and the Hebraic, the Greek and the Christian, or the Hebraic and the Christian which many moderns have believed inevitable and irreconcilable. Milton found, I believe, that the tragedies he most admired presented the suffering of a hero and perhaps his death. (*Samson Agonistes,* unlike *Oedipus the King* or *Philoctetes,* presents both.) At the end of the most moving of those tragedies, the hero was, whether alive or dead, in some sense "greater" than he was at the beginning. And the fate of the

hero involved the fate of a society and the imaginative reconciliation of the audience to that fate.

But Milton's choice of Samson as a tragic figure did make for
some differences from his Greek models and some problems.
Since Samson was a hero of the one God in a particularly Hebraic or Christian sense, the final triumph must be clear and
unambiguous. But if the movement of the drama were simply
from degradation and suffering to triumph, the audience might
view it with approval but without the raising of "pity and fear,
or terror," without the purgation which Milton believed essential
for tragedy. Milton solved the problems characteristically by the
creation of movements in events, ideas, emotions, perspectives,
and language, and he invented a new kind of verse. The movements of his drama are anything but simple; and, since they are
often ironical or paradoxical and simultaneous, they are easier
to experience than to describe. I wish here to point out only a
few of those movements which seem central to our experience
of the poem and which it is possible for good readers to miss.

With the opening soliloquy we recognize that this drama
"never was intended" for "the Stage" and that this is scarcely a
limitation: the hero is blind and in chains and he must be led;
the significant action will be largely within Samson's mind and
heart, and for that, language rather than gesture will be largely
sufficient. And yet we should also realize that there is an imaginary "stage" and that we will be compelled, at certain moments,
to imagine gestures which are of the greatest importance for
the internal drama. The opening lines provide an example: "A
little onward lend thy guiding hand/ To these dark steps, a

little further on." We must imagine the scene with action when Samson responds to Dalila's final wile ("Let me approach at least, and touch thy hand") with "Not for thy life, lest fierce remembrance wake/ My sudden rage to tear thee joint by joint"; or when Samson offers his last challenge to Harapha: "bring up thy van/ My heels are fetter'd, but my fist is free." The verse frequently suggests physical movement as well as attitude: when the Chorus approaches, we hear, "This, this is he; softly a while/ Let us not break in upon him"; and Dalila begins, "With doubtful feet and wavering resolution/ I came, still dreading thy displeasure, Samson."

More important, I believe, is our immediate recognition that if, in comparison to Adam before the Fall or the Christ of *Paradise Regained,* Samson is more nearly what we think of as "human," he is still not very much "like one of ourselves." The anguish of the opening soliloquy is as much below or beyond our ordinary experience as Samson's final assurance and divine possession will be above or beyond it. Samson is not a likeable hero; no one could wish to be this ruined sufferer. He is beyond the civilized and pleasant nonheroic values. He is near death, and his rage at his suffering is immense; yet he is possessed by his sense of divine mission, and he refuses the comforting idea that he is merely a victim. When we see such a figure we wish, like the choruses of many Greek tragedies, to cry out and to turn away our eyes.

Yet we also feel fascination with the terrible energy of his questions and his cries. We recognize an almost superhuman force not only in his expressions of suffering and despair but also in his ability to check them: "Yet stay," "But peace." And we recognize that the identity of this man is neither simple nor even continuous. Who *is* Samson? The question will reecho throughout the drama. At this point we recognize with Samson that what he is now is not what he was; and we feel, too, that this present being must change or cease. But we cannot define the "self" even of this moment. Is it the body which finds "some ease" in "This unfrequented place" or the mind, tormented with "restless thoughts," "like a deadly swarm/ Of hornets arm'd?" Does "impotence of mind in body strong" really describe the tormented self we hear? Or is another "self" implied by "Whom have I to complain of but myself?"—a spirit almost impossible to imagine as separate from the body and the mind yet larger than they, which here feels "amends" and later believes "that to mee Strength is my bane?" What is it that feels "Myself my Sepulcher, a moving Grave?"

Along with these movements and questionings, we are immediately engaged with the language, in which the multiple meanings and significant perspectives of images and statements and events are continually unfolded. The complexities concerning dark and light, sight and blindness, are introduced in Samson's opening soliloquy and continue throughout the drama. There are also weakness and strength, slavery and freedom, death and life. Before we have read far, we discover that this sort of doubleness is pervasive and is expressed in certain characteristic forms. There are paradoxes, reversals, and conscious ironies, but more unusual are the unconscious prophecies which are later discovered to be true in a sense which the speakers (and often, too, the audience) did not realize at the time when they were made. We discover by the end that the entire drama has been a representation of a "guiding hand" leading Samson "a little further on"; and we find that "The breath of Heav'n fresh-blowing, pure and sweet,/ With day-spring born" has truly been active at "yonder bank" before the prison in a sense which Samson has neither anticipated nor even dared to hope. Something similar occurs with Samson's conviction, "And I shall shortly be with them that rest." More individual still is the presentation of alternatives which seem mutually exclusive (either/or), both of which prove to be true. Manoa argues, "His might continues in thee not for naught,/ Nor shall his wondrous gifts be frustrate thus," and Samson replies, "All otherwise to me my thoughts portend,/ That these dark orbs no more shall treat with light,/ Nor th'other light of life continue long"; it is inconceivable to them that both should be right. In his final speech Samson prophesies, "This day will be remarkable in my life/ By some great act, or of my days the last." Somewhat similar in effect is the brief statement of likeness or simile which proves to be a statement of identity. When the members of the Chorus first view Samson, they remark that he lies "As one past hope, abandon'd,/ And by himself giv'n over." When Dalila approaches, "Some rich Philistian Matron she may seem." With the "hideous noise" of the catastrophe, the Chorus exclaims, "Noise call you it or universal groan/ As if the whole inhabitation perish'd?" Both the false either/or construction and the simile-become-identity occur together in the Messenger's description of Samson at the moment before he addresses the Philistines:

> with head a while inclin'd
> And eyes fast fixt he stood, as one who pray'd
> Or some great matter in his mind revolv'd.[1]   (1636–38)

We recognize that for the new Samson of this moment there can be no distinction between serious thought and prayer.

These evidences of "doubleness" do not invite or allow us to respond merely with a "mature" and static "wisdom." This is a drama, not a lyric. The chief problems and complexities with which we and Samson are concerned cannot be solved merely by soliloquy and "realization"; there must be action and change before this fearful blind sufferer can become the gymnast at the "theater," performing his Herculean labors playfully, and triumphantly and destructively wrestling with the pillars. The major action is occasioned by Samson's encounters with the Chorus, Manoa, Dalila, Harapha, and the Public Officer. Those exchanges may be thought of both as "debates" and as "temptations," but neither term alone adequately describes them. The Chorus and Manoa come as comforters, but they provide challenges and temptations, and they make Samson more determinedly wish for death. Dalila, that debating Circe, comes to seduce, and the Giant Harapha to "stare at" and "insult" a supposedly defeated and weakened and hopeless man; they both retire with some fear for their physical safety from a determined, fearless, and strengthened man. The Public Officer comes with a simple official order and receives a triple denial; when he returns and threatens violence, he achieves an unexpected compliance, a pyrrhic victory

---

[1] All my quotations are from the text of Merritt Y. Hughes, ed., *John Milton: Complete Poems and Major Prose* (New York, 1957).

for which, as Samson has warned him earlier, he shall "have cause to sorrow indeed." Each offers temptations or trials—often what seem merely repetitions or developments of ideas or emotions which Samson has formerly expressed. But the pattern of Samson's responses is not merely to reject the external temptation or to recognize and correct his own errors. He does more than preserve what he has achieved from external threats and more than merely recover his former status. With each episode he achieves a new position, a new strength, and finds himself in a place he has never been before. At the end he achieves fully for the first time the heroic self prophesied before his birth.

The achievement of a heroic self is by no means a process which makes either the hero or his audience feel consistently better and better. The conclusion of each episode finds Samson in some respects "stronger" or "greater" than before, yet he is more despairing after his meeting with Manoa than he was at the beginning. The finally triumphant self must possess trust in God, knowledge of himself and his mission, confidence in the possibility of action, and physical strength. But the movements of a fallen man toward such a self may be excruciating. With the initial episodes Samson advances in strength and insight in that he sees his own responsibility for his fall. He exonerates God from the charges of injustice and fickleness. He comes to see his present servitude, "These rags, this grinding," as

> not yet so base
> As was my former servitude, ignoble,
> Unmanly, ignominious, infamous,
> True slavery, and that blindness worse than this,
> That saw not how degenerately I serv'd.   (415–19)

But this spiritual advance involves an increase in psychological suffering. He sees the shame, the horror, the slavery as truly *his*. Samson is confident that the just and powerful God will triumph, but he believes that he can have no part in that triumph. He has failed God and he believes that God has abandoned him. Earlier he could feel amidst his suffering at least the affirmation of the self involved in his cries. Now he is naked; he can only wish for death. Dalila must first offer him a way of life which would imply the final acceptance of his sense of purposelessness, the death of his hope, before Samson comes to recognize that he will not accept the spiritual death of the self. And when Harapha insists that God has abandoned Samson, that He would not accept as His agent "A Murderer, a Revolter, and a Robber," Samson offers himself as God's champion. He is sure that, if the offer is rejected, it will be by Harapha and Dagon, not by God.

Each stage of Samson's transformation takes him further beyond ordinary, nonheroic experience. No one in the drama understands fully his decision to attend the Philistine festival. At his final action he is utterly alone except for God. Our difficulties in apprehending who this Samson is and how he changes and achieves his triumph increase as the action proceeds. It is, I believe, the Chorus, those other spectators and sufferers before the heroic action, who are closest to us and whose observations and responses are most helpful in directing our attention to the various movements, large and small. This is not at all to say that the Chorus is "right"; it is, rather, to recognize that the Chorus is often wrong in typically unheroic ways, and that only as a result of the action does it acquire "true experience" and understanding. Those Danites, friends and contemporaries of Samson, represent the "conventional wisdom" of the drama; but the premise of the poem is that conventional wisdom is inadequate for tragic experience. If it were otherwise, there would be no function for the tragedy; the community would already have been saved. And, although we are expected to see more than the Chorus—to see their errors—if our conventional wisdom as an audience were truly sufficient we should have nothing to learn from the imaginative reenactment of the drama.

The members of the Chorus come initially to comfort the fallen hero. But even before Samson hears their words, they move quickly from "Can this be hee,/ That Heroic, that Renown'd,/ Irresistible *Samson?*" to a lament for his blindness and his bondage, and an easy application of *vanitas:* "O mirror of our fickle state." When at last they speak directly to Samson, it soon becomes obvious that a good deal of irritant is mixed with their balm of consolation. When Samson laments the disproportion of his former strength and wisdom ("Those two proportion'd ill drove me transverse"), the Chorus reprimands him:

> Tax not divine disposal; wisest Men
> Have err'd, and by bad Women been deceived;
> And shall again, pretend they ne'er so wise.   (210–12)

They develop what is for them the major point: Does Samson still think he was essentially different from other men? He should not "Deject" himself "so overmuch" for common human frailty; he should, at last, admit that his former claims to particular divine impulsion were mistaken. Had he not broken the tribal code and married outside the Israelitish nation, he could, supposedly, have been as one of his comforters: observing the fickleness of man's fate, lamenting the communal oppression, but without any specific private deed for which he must lament or take responsibility.

But Samson is not so submissive as the Chorus has assumed. He refuses to deny either his inspiration or his responsibility:

> The first I saw at Timna, and she pleas'd
> Mee, not my parents, that I sought to wed,
> The daughter of an Infidel: they knew not
> That what I motion'd was of God; I knew
> From intimate impulse . . .   (219–23)

Dalila he regrets (he had acted there without specific inspiration), but he refuses to place the responsibility of his failure on her: "of what now I suffer/ She was not the prime cause, but I myself."

The implications of the Chorus' response, "Yet *Israel* still serves with all his Sons," are obvious: Samson's life has been futile and his claims for extraordinary inspiration have been disproved by what has happened. Samson turns to the attack:

> That fault I take not on me, but transfer
> On *Israel's* Governors, and Heads of Tribes. (241–42)

At Etham, "Had *Judah* that day join'd, or one whole Tribe" Israel would have been freed. The charge is specific: the failure was each tribe's. And the members of the Chorus are precisely those "friends and equals" of Samson, the alternative warriors and leaders of his own tribe of Dan, who might have been expected to feel a greater responsibility than any others to support their champion. The charge is not at all softened by Samson's famous lines on the characteristic behavior of corrupt nations who prefer "Bondage with ease" to "strenuous liberty"; who despise, envy, suspect, and desert their heroic deliverers, and then "heap ingratitude on worthiest deeds." The comforters who have come to console (and to welcome to the ranks of the unheroic) a defeated and supposedly abject hero suddenly find themselves charged with their own lack of heroism. They take refuge in generalizations and historical analogies—Gideon and Jephtha: such actions have indeed happened in the past. But Samson will not let them off so easily: "Of such examples add me to the roll." The true crime is not the neglect of Samson but of God's "propos'd deliverance."

This is the moment of the Chorus' expostulation, "Just are the ways of God," to be followed by "Down Reason then, at least vain reasonings down." In the context, the ironies are obvious. They refuse to face the charge that Samson has made concerning their own responsibility in the continuing captivity of Israel. Instead, they have gone back to Samson's impressive claim that he was divinely inspired to break the marriage laws. They are no longer concerned with the fate of the nation but with the shocking suggestions that God is not tied to ceremonial law, that God may suspend or destroy "National obscription," that God's hero may not be judged accurately or finally by the laws of the community. They cling to the doctrine of the justice of God, but their faith is truly blind. They do not understand. They can perceive no pattern or purpose.

In the painful scene with Manoa, Samson gently reprimands his father for the most bitter charges against God in the drama and demonstrates God's justice in his own fate with a precision alien to the Chorus. His dishonor to God's cause is now his "chief affliction, shame and sorrow,/ The anguish of my Soul." When he says, "His pardon I implore; but as for Life,/ To what end should I seek it?" and expresses his self-contempt, the Chorus can only break in with a hymn to Samson's abstinence from wine and "strongest drinks"; but they are speechless when Samson, agreeing in the celebration of this temperance, asks, "But what avail'd this temperance, not complete/ Against another object more enticing?" They are deeply moved by Samson's expression of ultimate torment, "swoonings of despair,/ And sense of Heav'n's desertion," and by his "one prayer"—"speedy death"; and they then recognize their own inadequacy and ignorance. They realize that the traditional wisdom "Extolling Patience as the truest fortitude" is irrelevant to the suffering that they see and hear. Before a sufferer can make use of that wisdom, he must be above despair, he must "feel within/ Some source of consolation from above;/ Secret refreshings, that repair his strength,/ And fainting spirits uphold." Helpless, they turn to honest expostulation: "God of our Fathers, what is man!" They face directly the incommensurable appearances of God's actions, the "unseemly falls in human eyes,/ Too grievous for the trespass or omission" of his heroes. And their account of the various "evil ends" to which the heroes are subjected raises the question of what death is becoming for the hero. If he escapes a fall at his height, death or exile from his enemies, condemnation from "th' ingrateful multitude" whom he has served, is a later fall into "poverty/ With sickness and disease" any more "just?" Is "crude old age" a consummation to be wished?

They end with a prayer. They do not know even what to ask. Their initial petition, "So deal not with this once thy glorious Champion,/ The Image of thy strength, and mighty minister," is suddenly undercut by "What do I beg? how hast thou dealt already?" They cannot believe that the unjust fate has not already occurred; they cannot really imagine an alternative. But their prayer ends with the request that God should *look* at Samson:

> Behold him in this state calamitous, and turn
> His labors, for thou canst, to peaceful end.   (708-9)

They are convinced of God's power beyond their own imaginations. They retain their faith; it is all that they have left.

This is one of the most significant turning points of the drama. At this moment we share an immediate insight with the Chorus: the resolution lies within the will of God. And, as imaginative spectators at the tragedy, we are also convinced that, with *this* Samson, God must behold. For the salvation of the community, for the satisfaction of this humble and blind faith, Samson's "calamitous state" must be changed; his spirit must be restored, his sense of purpose revived, and his destiny fulfilled. The rest of the drama provides the answer to the prayer.

Dalila's approach seems an interruption, but it begins the answer. The members of the Chorus, like a number of the commentators on the poem, seem strangely imperceptive in their response to the scene with Dalila. They miss the contradictions between her various justifications (weakness, love, religion, and patriotism); miss the facts that, in her desire to make Samson "Mine and Love's prisoner," she is the prototype of the woman who wishes to reduce her lover to an object totally within her power, and that her argument would justify any woman's maiming and enslaving any lover who wished to engage in heroic action—or even leave the house. They miss, too, Samson's most profound distinction between love and lust: "Love seeks to have Love"—not merely the lover. They cannot understand that "All wickedness is weakness." Only at the end, when Dalila expresses her satisfaction with her role as Philistine heroine, does the Chorus recognize her as "a manifest Serpent." They then turn to what they have perceived (the "inward passion" which Samson's violence has manifested) and to what they are best at, generalization—this time concerning the mystery of woman's love and the misery it causes man. Like Adam after the Fall and like traditional misogynous literature ever since, they would like to place all the blame for the failures and the misery on woman. The last two sections of their ode seem to me the most syntactically difficult passages in the poem. The final lines concerning "God's universal Law" that "Gave to the man despotic power" seem to imply once again that it was Dalila who was truly the cause of Samson's fall, and that it was Samson's mistake not to be despotic enough in his relationship to her. But just before, seemingly unconscious of the differing implications, they have stated:

> But virtue which breaks through all opposition,
> And all temptation can remove,
> Most shines and most is acceptable above. (1050–52)

We can recognize that one of the most heroic human actions may be to recover from subjection, to achieve triumphant purpose despite defeat in love and betrayal.

After their generalized consideration of heroism in love, the members of the Chorus perceive Harapha as an approaching storm and suggest that both they and Samson should retire. They respond with initial delight to Samson's recovery of confidence and his verbal victory over the "tongue-doughty Giant": "His Giantship is gone somewhat crestfall'n." But they are immediately concerned with his "sultry chafe," and they fear the result of Samson's momentary triumph:

> He will directly to the Lords, I fear,
> And with malicious counsel stir them up
> Some way or other yet further to afflict thee.
>
> (1250–52)

But Samson, strong now in mind as well as body, has no fear. He can calculate the possibilities, but he is sure that nothing that Harapha or the Philistines can do can hurt him. Although he still desires death ("The worst that he can give, to me the best"), he no longer believes his fate negligible. And there is more than a desire for death in his grim recognition of the "ruin" that may await the "friends" who attempt to give him his desire. To his confidence the Chorus responds with "Oh how comely it is and how reviving/ To the Spirits of just men long opprest!" They imagine the moment when "God into the hands of their deliverer/ Puts invincible might," when the hero triumphs over the usual material means of the enemy "With plain Heroic magnitude of mind/ And celestial vigor arm'd." This is the moment they have desired and this the hero that, for a moment, they believe they have glimpsed. Now, after Samson's encounters with Dalila and Harapha and his new confidence, the Chorus knows that Samson is a hero and will achieve a hero's "end." But they remember that there is another sort of hero:

> But patience is more oft the exercise
> Of Saints, the trial of their fortitude,
> Making them each his own Deliverer,
> And Victor over all
> That tyranny or fortune can inflict.
> Either of these is in thy lot,
> *Samson,* with might endu'd
> Above the Sons of men; but sight bereav'd
> May chance to number thee with those
> Whom Patience finally must crown.   (1287-96)

They assume that the active and the suffering heroes are always differing individuals, that the two forms can never be united; and they assume, despite their hope, that Samson's heroism will be of the second kind. But a major point of Milton's Christian tragedy (and of his thought elsewhere) is that the active hero is only truly heroic if he has first triumphed over "all/ That tyranny or fortune can inflict." Every hero is a hero of patience. The question whether the patiently crowned heroism shall proceed to active public deliverance depends upon the will of God.

By Samson's brief encounter with the Public Officer and his triple refusal to attend the festival ("I cannot come," "I will not come," "I will not come"), the Chorus, unheroic even if able to glimpse heroism, is alarmed. They advise worldly and fearful wisdom: "Consider Samson; matters now are strain'd/ Up to the height, whether to hold or break." When Samson asks, "Shall I abuse this Consecrated gift/ Of strength, again returning with my hair/ After my great transgression, so requite/ Favor renew'd, and add a greater sin/ By prostituting holy things to Idols?" the Chorus replies, "Yet with this strength thou serv'st the *Philistines,*/ Idolatrous, uncircumcis'd, unclean." Convinced with difficulty that God may dispense with ceremonial observances or communal laws for specific men and purposes, the Chorus now develops that doctrine for the unheroic purpose of avoiding trouble. To attend and participate in the festival of Dagon would be only one *other* way of serving the Philistines; and to do so under "force" would be no sin at all: "Where the heart joins not, outward acts defile not." Samson violently uncovers the sophistry:

> Where outward force constrains, the sentence holds;
> But who constrains me to the Temple of Dagon,
> Not dragging? the *Philistian* Lords command.
> Commands are no constraints. If I obey them,
> I do it freely; venturing to displease
> God for the fear of Man, and Man prefer,
> Set God behind: which in his jealousy
> Shall never, unrepented, find forgiveness.
> Yet that he may dispense with me or thee
> Present in Temples at Idolatrous Rites
> For some important cause, thou needst not doubt.

$$(1369-79)$$

Heroic freedom is not the ability to do great actions without getting hurt. Samson will not break the ceremonial law, will not make sport of his person "with blind activity," will not "play before their gods" because of fear or apparent physical "constraint"; but he also serves notice that, should God inspire him with a sense of purpose and possibility, he will not be constrained by the traditions and the ceremonial laws of Israel.

The Chorus is defeated. They can no longer advise the hero: "How thou wilt here come off surmounts my reach." But their use of "come off" implies their sense of "get away with it," "come off" with one's skin intact. And now the initial roles of Samson and the Chorus are completely reversed; Samson comforts them with his new resolution and a prophecy:

> Be of good courage, I begin to feel
> Some rousing motions in me which dispose
> To something extraordinary my thoughts.
> I with this Messenger will go along,
> Nothing to do, be sure, that may dishonor
> Our Law, or stain my vow of *Nazarite*.
> If there be aught of presage in the mind,
> This day will be remarkable in my life
> By some great act, or of my day the last.   (1381-89)

The Chorus does not respond to the new ring of confidence which we hear in Samson's voice. They seem to take his decision as evidence that Samson has at last shown that he is as they are; that, whether he will admit it or not, he has followed the logic of their arguments and will here "come off" with self-protective temporizing: "In time thou hast resolved, the man returns." Samson's response to the Officer's ultimatum indicates that he has perceived the unheroic appearance of his decision. His heavy irony is surely directed both at the Chorus and at the Officer:

> Yet knowing thir advantages too many
> Because they shall not trail me through thir streets
> Like a wild Beast, I am content to go.
> Master's commands come with a power resistless
> To such as owe them absolute subjection;
> And for a life who will not change his purpose?
> (So mutable are all the ways of men).   (1401–7)

But in Samson's parody of those incapable of heroism we can glimpse a more profound irony. "Master's commands come with a power resistless/ To such as owe them absolute subjection" seems to apply to Samson's position as Hebrew slave to the Philistines, and Samson intends that it should seem so. But we know that Samson does not owe "absolute subjection" to any nation or person; he owes it only to God; and we see (or will come to see) that those "rousing motions" have come as a command from that "master." And the ultimate surface cynicism of "And for a life who will not change his purpose?/ (So mutable are all the ways of men)" also has an additional and deeper dimension. The rhetorical question raises swiftly the true question of what *is* "a life," and takes us back to the earlier exchange with the Officer when, after Samson's second refusal, the Officer had said, "Regard thyself, this will offend them highly." Then, Samson had replied,

> Myself? my conscience and internal peace.
> Can they think me so broken, so debas'd
> With corporal servitude, that my mind ever
> Will condescend to such absurd comands? (1334–37)

Samson has changed his "purpose" with extraordinary swiftness; he has done so in response to a "Master's" command, "Come with a power resistless"; and, not at all in the sense which the Chorus and the Officer understand, he has done so "for a life."

In his farewell to the Chorus Samson directs no irony toward them. He dismisses them with an almost paternal concern for their welfare, and again he comforts them:

> Happen what may, of me expect to hear
> Nothing dishonorable, impure, unworthy
> Our God, our Law, my Nation, or myself;
> The last of me or no I cannot warrant. (1423–26)

The response of the Chorus is rapt: "Go, and the Holy One/ Of Israel be thy guide/ To what may serve his glory best." Increasingly toward the end of the drama, as they respond to the events and remember the prophecies, the members of the Chorus are inspired by a sense of purpose beyond their conscious knowledge. In the scene with Manoa after Samson's departure, everyone is waiting. But with the "hideous noise," it is the Chorus which reproves Manoa's alarm with "Thy Son is rather slaying them." And it is the Chorus which first imagines the deliverance:

> What if his eyesight (for to *Israel's* God
> Nothing is hard) by miracle restor'd,
> He now be dealing dole among his foes? (1527–29)

After the Messenger's marvelous narration of the catastrophe, it is the Chorus, both understanding and inspired, which chants the celebration of the victory and its meaning. Manoa interrupts with "Come, come, no time for lamentation now"—although the Chorus has not been lamenting. He, too, understands that there should be no sorrow for Samson's death. Yet, as he describes the funeral ceremony to come, the monument, the continued life of Samson "In copious Legend, or sweet Lyric Song" and in the inspiration which his story will provide the "valiant youth," he still imagines that the Virgins of Sion will have one thing to lament: "His lot unfortunate in nuptial choice/ From whence captivity and loss of eyes." It is the Chorus, in inspired reprimand to Manoa, which extends the affirmation to the universal: "All is best." The mystery has been revealed; God's Champion has been justified; the members of the Chorus (and we, the audience) have suffered and have come to knowledge. Nothing is to be lamented, nothing to be desired.

All the significant movements of the drama are centered in the destiny of Samson. But the destiny of a chosen and fallen hero of God involves not merely the "recognition" but the recreation of the self; and it must be manifested in action which, making evident the will of God, transforms the hero's world. Radically individual, its significance must be experienced both by the members of the hero's society and by those later individuals who attend the dramatic re-creation of the action. There is no simple formula for such a destiny. However "mythic" or traditional in its details, it is worked out within the time and the limitations of an individual human life. And however great the faith or knowledge of either the hero or the onlookers, no one can predict the ways in which strength will be repossessed and triumph achieved. The final triumph implies not an obliteration or denial of degradation and suffering and death, but an anguished and ecstatic acceptance of even those horrors which, in the final revelation, have proved significant. *Samson Agonistes* concludes with the celebration of Samson's life and death; but that acceptance of "all" and of the end of desire for Samson implies that, for the Chorus and the audience, significant movements and actions may again begin.

SUPERVISING COMMITTEE

THE ENGLISH INSTITUTE, 1964

THE PROGRAM
SEPTEMBER 8 THROUGH
SEPTEMBER 11, 1964

II. *THOUGHT AND IMAGINATION IN EIGHTEENTH-CENTURY LITERATURE*

DIRECTED BY REUBEN A. BROWER, HARVARD UNIVERSITY

1. Intellectual History and the Literary Critic

DONALD GREENE, VICTORIA COLLEGE, UNIVERSITY OF TORONTO

2. Augustanism and Seventeenth-Century Ethics

WILLIAM YOUNGREN, MASSACHUSETTS INSTITUTE OF TECHNOLOGY

3. The Poetry of Rhetoric

PHILLIP HARTH, NORTHWESTERN UNIVERSITY

4. Pictures and Powers: Voice and Image in the Sublime Poem

MARTIN PRICE, YALE UNIVERSITY

III. *LITERARY HISTORY AND OTHER DISCIPLINES: THE CASE OF VICTORIAN ENGLAND*

DIRECTED BY MICHAEL WOLFF, INDIANA UNIVERSITY

1. The Uses of Context: Aspects of the 1860s

MICHAEL WOLFF, INDIANA UNIVERSITY

2. Psychological Depths and Dover Beach

NORMAN N. HOLLAND, MASSACHUSETTS INSTITUTE OF TECHNOLOGY

3. Moral Problems and Moral Philosophy in the Victorian Period

J. B. SCHNEEWIND, UNIVERSITY OF PITTSBURGH

IV. *THE MINORITY VOICE IN AMERICAN WRITING*

DIRECTED BY R. W. B. LEWIS, YALE UNIVERSITY

1. The Novel as Protest

LESLIE A. FIEDLER, MONTANA STATE UNIVERSITY

2. The Novel of Outrage: Minorities in Recent American Fiction

IHAB HASSAN, WESLEYAN UNIVERSITY

3. *The Conversions of the Jews*
   ALLEN GUTTMANN, AMHERST COLLEGE

EVENING MEETING, SEPTEMBER *10*
   Reading from Work in Progress
   RALPH ELLISON, NEW YORK CITY

liams University; Mary Campbell Brill, Madison College; James H. Broderick, Cynwyd, Pennsylvania; Reuben A. Brower, Harvard University; Stephen J. Brown, The George Washington University; Audrey Bruné, Sir George Williams University; Margaret M. Bryant, Brooklyn College; Mrs. W. Bryher, Vavd, Switzerland; Jean R. Buchert, University of North Carolina (Greensboro); Janet Buck, Douglass College; Robert B. Burlin, Bryn Mawr College; Sister M. Vincentia Burns, Albertus Magnus College; David Burrows, Douglass College; Katherine Burton, Wheaton College; Douglas Bush, Harvard University; George E. Bush, Jr., St. John's University; Mervin Butovsky, Sir George Williams University; Grace J. Calder, Hunter College; Edward F. Callahan, College of the Holy Cross; Kenneth Neill Cameron, The Carl H. Pforzheimer Library; Sister Eileen Campion, College of St. Elizabeth; James Card, Franklin and Marshall College; Gale H. Carrithers, Jr., State University of New York (Buffalo); Sister Mary Charles, Immaculata College; Hugh C. G. Chase, Bristol, New Hampshire; James L. Clifford, Columbia University; C. L. Cline, University of Texas; Arthur Collins, State University of New York (Albany); Alice P. Comparetti, Colby College; Ralph W. Condee, Pennsylvania State University; Allen Blow Cook, U.S. Naval Academy; Thomas W. Copeland, University of Massachusetts; Homer T. Cox, University of Waterloo; G. Armour Craig, Amherst College; James H. Croushore, Mary Washington College; Cornelius J. Crowley, St. Louis University; Frances G. Crowley, University of Missouri (Normandy); Margaret Croyden, Jersey City State College; J. V. Cunningham, Brandeis University; Curtis Dahl, Wheaton College; Elizabeth A. Daniels, Vassar College; Arthur P. Davis, Howard University; Charles T. Davis, Pennsylvania State University; Winifred M. Davis, The Carl H. Pforzheimer Library; Douglas Day, University of Virginia; Robert A. Day, Queens College; Sara de Ford, Goucher College; Sister Anne Cyril Delaney, Emmanuel College; E. Talbot Donaldson, Yale University; John H. Dorenkamp, Holy Cross College; Marjorie Downing, Sarah Law-

Matthew Grace, Emory University; the Reverend Thomas J. Grace, s.j., Holy Cross College; James Gray, Bishop's University; Donald J. Greene, University of Toronto; M. E. Grenander, State University of New York (Albany); Mother Pauline Grindon, Maryville College; Edward Groff, Lincoln University; Allen Guttmann, Amherst College; Jean H. Hagstrum, Northwestern University; Lawrence S. Hall, Bowdoin College; Robert G. Hallwachs, Wells College; Violet B. Halpert, Brooklyn Polytechnic Institute; Robert Halsband, Columbia University; Victor M. Hamm, Marquette University; Reginald L. Hannaford, Bowdoin College; Richard C. Harrier, New York University; Victor Harris, Brandeis University; Francis R. Hart, University of Virginia; John A. Hart, Carnegie Institute of Technology; Phillip Harth, Northwestern University; Joan E. Hartman, Connecticut College; Ihab Hassan, Wesleyan University; Ann L. Hayes, Carnegie Institute of Technology; Mary E. Hazard, Philadelphia; Patrick D. Hazard, Beaver College; Allen T. Hazen, Columbia University; Donald Scott Heines, Upsala College; Neil H. Hertz, Cornell University; the Reverend William Bernard Hill, s.j., Novitiate of St. Isaac Jogues; F. W. Hilles, Yale University; Haskell Hinnant, Columbia University; C. Fenno Hoffman, Jr., Rhode Island School of Design; Daniel Hoffman, Swarthmore College; Stanley M. Holberg, St. Lawrence University; Laurence B. Holland, Princeton University; Norman N. Holland, Massachusetts Institute of Technology; John Hollander, Yale University; Vivian C. Hopkins, State University of New York (Albany); Florence Howe, Goucher College; Muriel J. Hughes, University of Vermont; Clay Hunt, Williams College; Eleanor N. Hutchens, Agnes Scott College; Julia Hysham, Skidmore College; William A. Jamison, Houghton Mifflin Co.; Mackie Jarrell, Connecticut College; Sears Jayne, City University of New York (Queens); George W. Johnson, Temple University; James William Johnson, University of Rochester; Wendell Stacy Johnson, Hunter College; Leah E. Jordan, West Chester State College; Sister M. Joselyn, College of St. Scholastica;

Sister Julie, Rosary College; R. J. Kaufmann, University of Rochester; John E. Keating, Kent State University; Mary A. Keelan, University of Chicago; Robert Kellogg, University of Virginia; James G. Kennedy, Upsala College; Sighle Kennedy, Hunter College; Anne R. King, Adelphi University; H. L. Kleinfield, C. W. Post College; Carl F. Klinck, University of Western Ontario; Edwin B. Knowles, Pratt Institute; Stanley Koehler, University of Massachusetts; Kathrine Koller, University of Rochester; Maurice Kramer, Brooklyn College; Frank A. Krutzke, Colorado College; Jay D. Kugelman, University of Rochester; Lincoln F. Ladd, Duke University; the Reverend John P. Lahey, s.j., Le Moyne College; Gordon Lameyer, University of New Hampshire; S. S. Lamb, Sir George Williams University; Roy Lamson, Massachusetts Institute of Technology; Lewis Leary, Columbia University; Albert Leet, Franklin and Marshall College; George Levine, Indiana University; R. W. B. Lewis, Yale University; Ellen Douglass Leyburn, Agnes Scott College; H. W. Liebert, Yale University Library; Eleanor T. Lincoln, Smith College; David L. Littlefield, Middlebury College; George DeF. Lord, Yale University; Mother Marie-Louise, College of New Rochelle; Winslow H. Loveland, Boston University; J. P. Lovering, Canisius College; Marion K. Mabey, Wells College; Isabel G. MacCaffrey, Bryn Mawr College; Richard A. Macksey, The Johns Hopkins University; Hugh N. MacLean, State University of New York (Albany); Lorna E. MacLean, Sir George Williams University; William G. Madsen, Emory University; Mother C. E. Maguire, Newton College of the Sacred Heart; C. F. Main, Rutgers University; Robert Marsh, State University of New York (Stony Brook); Thomas F. Marshall, Kent State University; Edward A. Martin, Middlebury College; Harold C. Martin, Harvard University; Louis L. Martz, Yale University; Dorothy Mateer, The College of Wooster; John K. Mathison, University of Wyoming; Donald C. Mell, Jr., Rutgers University; John H. Middendorf, Columbia University; Milton Millhauser, University of Bridgeport; the Reverend Joseph

The New School; Sister Cor Mariae Schuler, Marymount Manhattan College; H. T. Schultz, Dartmouth College; Nayda M. Schultz, Waterloo Lutheran University; Merton M. Sealts, Jr., Lawrence University; Susan Field Senneff, Smith College; Richard Sexton, Fordham University; John T. Shawcross, Douglass College; Robert E. Shoenberg, Williams College; Agnes Sibley, Lindenwood College; Norman Silverstein, Queens College; Sister Agatha Smith, Marymount Manhattan College; Nelle Smither, Douglass College; George Soule, Carleton College; J. Gordon Spaulding, University of British Columbia; Nathan C. Starr, University of Florida; Sister M. Stephanie, St. Joseph's College; David L. Stevenson, Hunter College; Keith Stewart, University of Cincinnati; Margaret Stokes, New York City; Albert E. Stone, Jr., Emory University; Maureen T. Sullivan, Albertus Magnus College; Joseph H. Summers, Washington University (St. Louis); Barbara Swain, Vassar College; Anne R. Taylor, Brown University; E. William Terwilliger, Ithaca College; Jonathan Thomas, Douglass College; Wright Thomas, New York State University College (Cortland); Mother Thomas Aquinas, College of New Rochelle; Sister Thomas Marion, Nazareth College of Rochester; Richard J. Thompson, Canisius College; Donald Tritschler, Skidmore College; Susan J. Turner, Vassar College; Thomas F. Van Laan, Rutgers University; David M. Vieth, Hunter College; Howard P. Vincent, Kent State University; Sister M. Vivien, Caldwell College for Women; Eugene M. Waith, Yale University; Andrew J. Walker, Georgia Institute of Technology; A. Dayle Wallace, Wayne State University; M. Elizabeth Waterston, University of Western Ontario; Herbert Weil, Jr., University of Connecticut; David R. Weimer, Rutgers University; Mother Elizabeth White, Newton College of the Sacred Heart; Brother Joseph Wiesenfarth, Manhattan College; Autrey Nell Wiley, Texas Woman's University; Elizabeth Wiley, Susquehanna University; Roger B. Wilkenfeld, University of Connecticut; Zara Wilkenfield, University of Connecticut; Maurita Willett, University of Illinois; Mother Margaret Williams, Manhattan-